It Made My Heart Thump

Two other books by the same people,
published by Morning Walk Press:

We Felt Their Kindliness:
An American Family's Afghan Odyssey 1949–1951

We Stood in Awe:
Rebecca's Travel Diaries 1949 and 1953

All income from these books will be donated
to the American Friends Service Committee,
or will be used to publish and market
additional copies of the books.

time someone used the microwave, the deer entered the store, went to the microwave, and begged for pizza, hotdogs, or whatever. This was unacceptable.

We approached the deer and got a better look. It got up and greeted us with a few licks and a wagging tail. It was Bert.

We opened the animal carrier on the truck and told Bert to get in. He did, and we took him home with us, where he still resides today.

It was a beautiful sunny morning, with a chill in the air and a slight breeze blowing. We set the crate on a small hill above a flowing brook we could hear in the near silence. We opened the crate and left the door swinging open, then quietly backed away. For several minutes nothing happened. Finally a little deer head popped out the door. He slowly made his way out and just stood and looked around, sniffing the air. This beautiful animal would not have been alive if we had not intervened. He started walking down the hill and stopped about halfway to the bottom. He turned his head and looked back at us. We could see his tiny button antlers gleaming in the sun. Then he broke into a trot down the hill. He crossed through the draw, went up the other side, and disappeared into the woods. It was totally quiet again except for the sound of the brook.

It Made My Heart Thump

Rebecca's Letters from Iran
1951–1953

Based on the writings and photographs of
Rebecca Shannon Cresson and Osborne Coates Cresson

Edited by Os Cresson

Morning Walk Press
Iowa City, Iowa

Morning Walk Press, Iowa City, IA

oscresson1@gmail.com
ISBN: 978-0-9914344-2-8
Printed on acid-free paper

Cover: Wetherill, Os and Rebecca on the ruins of Ecbatana, capital of the Medes, with the city of Hamadan, Iran, below them.
Back cover: Rebecca and the children, and their taxi driver, in Hamadan, Iran. (See pp. 203, 31, 67, 161, and 204.)

Contents

School

Scenes Of Iranian Life

Travels

Acknowledgments

First of all, I am grateful to the Iranians Rebecca met who responded so warmly to her offer of friendship. This shines out to us in her writing.

This book is dedicated to five wonderful women, three you meet on these pages and two who were yet to come: Rebecca Edwards Shannon, Rebecca Shannon Cresson, Rebecca Wetherill Cresson Winder, Rebecca Shannon Winder and Rebecca Claire Lucienne Tanager.

Finally, my thanks go out to two people who particularly helped in getting this book done: Rebecca Winder and Sara T. Sauers.

Note From The Editor

This book is almost entirely Rebecca's words. The source materials are handwritten diaries, letters (mostly to her mother for recopying and mailing to friends), articles, and short stories.

As the editor, I made small changes to correct errors, smooth awkward places, and organize the material into a coherent scheme. Specifically, single words were changed on occasion, for instance where she used the same word twice in a sentence. Punctuation was altered where it is confusing or awkward, and the sequence of some of the sentences was changed (she sometimes thought of and wrote a sentence that belonged earlier in the text). When more than one word was added, these are in brackets, such as "[After returning from the bazaar]". Ellipsis (...) were not used to show where material was deleted. Changes were not made that would have to be repeated throughout the passage, such as a change of verb tense.

I sometimes combined several descriptions Rebecca wrote of the same event, as in a diary, letter, and article. In that case, all the documents are listed as the source of the passage. Sources are given on the right at the beginning of an excerpt.

Rebecca's diaries and letters were written rapidly and not edited. She used minimal punctuation and that practice has been followed here as much as possible. It helps convey the breathless quality of her writing. I tried not to intrude on her words, but to make the changes she would have made to produce an easily readable text.

Explanatory material and my personal recollections are in brackets or footnotes, and there is a glossary in the back of the book with Persian words Rebecca used frequently.

The source materials for this book, along with Rebecca's other writings, are in the "Rebecca S. Cresson Papers" at Friends Historical Library of Swarthmore College.

Preface

Rebecca and Osborne Cresson were pacifists who lived during two great wars. In 1949 they were looking for a way to help build a more peaceful and loving world. One way would be to live as neighbors with people of a different culture. This led them to Afghanistan for two years, and then to Iran for what would be two more years. When we moved from Kabul to Tehran in 1951, my sister, Wetherill, and I were ten and nine years old.[1]

In Tehran, Rebecca (who was 41 years old) and Osborne (46) taught in the Community School while Wetherill and I began 5th to 6th grades. The school had 500 students from 31 countries in 12 grades and was part of the Presbyterian Mission. For more than a century the Mission had been working on projects in education, health, handcrafts, publications and religious instruction. The main church in Tehran had about 1000 members, one third of Assyrian Christian origin, one third Armenian Christian, and one third converts from Islam or Judaism.[2]

Rebecca and Osborne were not missionaries, even though they worked for the Presbyterian Board of Foreign Missions. They were happy to answer questions about their Quaker faith but did not initiate these conversations. They tried to be supportive of all people searching for a path.

Rebecca loved to write and she produced letters, diaries and magazine articles. She wrote in a hurry, distracted by children and visitors, with a job at the school and volunteer duties, a husband with his own job, and health problems (her own and those of others) – all of this in a part of the world that was new to her. Osborne helped by taking pictures.

In Iran, Rebecca saw old traditions disappearing and new ones

1. Our full names at the time were Rebecca Wetherill Cresson and Osborne Coates Cresson, Jr. We are now Wetherill Cresson Winder and Osborn Cresson. (I simplified my name while living in Costa Rica for many years.) Wetherill and her husband, John Bovey, and I are living contentedly in Oaknoll Retirement Community in Iowa City, Iowa.

2. For more of the history of this dynamic enterprise since 1834, see: *History of the American Presbyterian Mission to Iran 1834-1960*, compiled by John Elder, Tehran: Literature Committee of the Christian Council of Iran, [n.d.].

taking their place. Her focus was on people who were involved in the changes rather than on an analysis of what was happening. She summed up her approach in a draft for an article:

> *We Went to School in Tehran*
>
> As has happened repeatedly in history, the eyes of the world are on Iran today. They chart political moves and judge the results but they miss so much: the subtlety and humor, the appealing lightheartedness and generosity which we learned to appreciate when we lived in Iran. We experienced the friendliness of Iran's people in many parts of the country, learned something of her folkways, and a little of her language. In spite of occasional crises, much of our life in Iran seemed very ordinary and why should it not, for even troublous days such as these are a small and oft repeated part of 4,000 years of recorded history.

It was a stressful time in Iran. The government nationalized the oil industry on March 15, 1951, three months before we arrived. Shah Mohammed Reza Pahlavi struggled with communists, religious conservatives and moderate reformers. Two months after we left in 1953, he was forced to abdicate and leave the country. A coup was quickly organized by the U.S. Central Intelligence Agency and the Shah returned and ruled for 25 years until the revolution of 1979.

Despite the political situation, life went on. Their lives were a delightful and exhausting mix of responsibilities and opportunities. Rebecca and Osborne made friends with school students, parents and staff, and missionaries (secular and evangelical), and people working in governmental and nongovernmental aid projects, and many others as they moved about Tehran and traveled farther out into Iran.

Our experience in Iran was similar to and different from our experience in Afghanistan, and this is reflected in Rebecca's writing. In Afghanistan she wrote about the amazing world around her and the challenges of living there. She was teaching at home and entertaining Osborne's Afghan students who came by almost daily. In Iran she had a job outside the home and when at home there were two extra children in the family and frequent visitors for meals and overnight.

There were still adventures like the ones we had in Afghanistan but these were now mixed with everyday elements similar to our lives in the U.S.: for instance, a Studebaker taxi took us from Tehran, the modern capital of Iran, to Ecbatana, the capital of the Medes 2600 years ago.

In this book I have collected Rebecca's writings and Osborne's pictures to show something of our lives in Iran, with a few explanatory comments in brackets and footnotes. The story begins as the family organizes the move from Kabul to Tehran. This is followed by an introduction to Tehran, and chapters on our family and expanding household. Then there are descriptions of our various activities, and the school where we worked and studied, and the people and places we encountered while traveling in Iran.[3]

This is a story of what can happen when we seek peace by living with people who seem different from us, committing to the proposition that goodwill toward others will carry us through any difficulty. Rebecca and Osborne opened their hearts to the Iranian people and they responded in kind. I hope their example will encourage others to do the same.

Os Cresson
Iowa City, IA
October 10, 2019

3. This book continues the story of our two years in Afghanistan described in: Os Cresson, ed., *We Felt Their Kindliness: An American Family's Afghan Odyssey 1949-1951* (1st edition, Haddonfield, NJ: Emerald Pademelon Press, 2003; 2nd edition, Iowa City, IA: Morning Walk Press, 2019). Our travels from New Mexico to Afghanistan, and from Iran to America, are described in: Os Cresson, ed., *We Stood in Awe: Rebecca's Travel Diaries 1949 and 1953* (Iowa City, IA: Morning Walk Press, 2020).

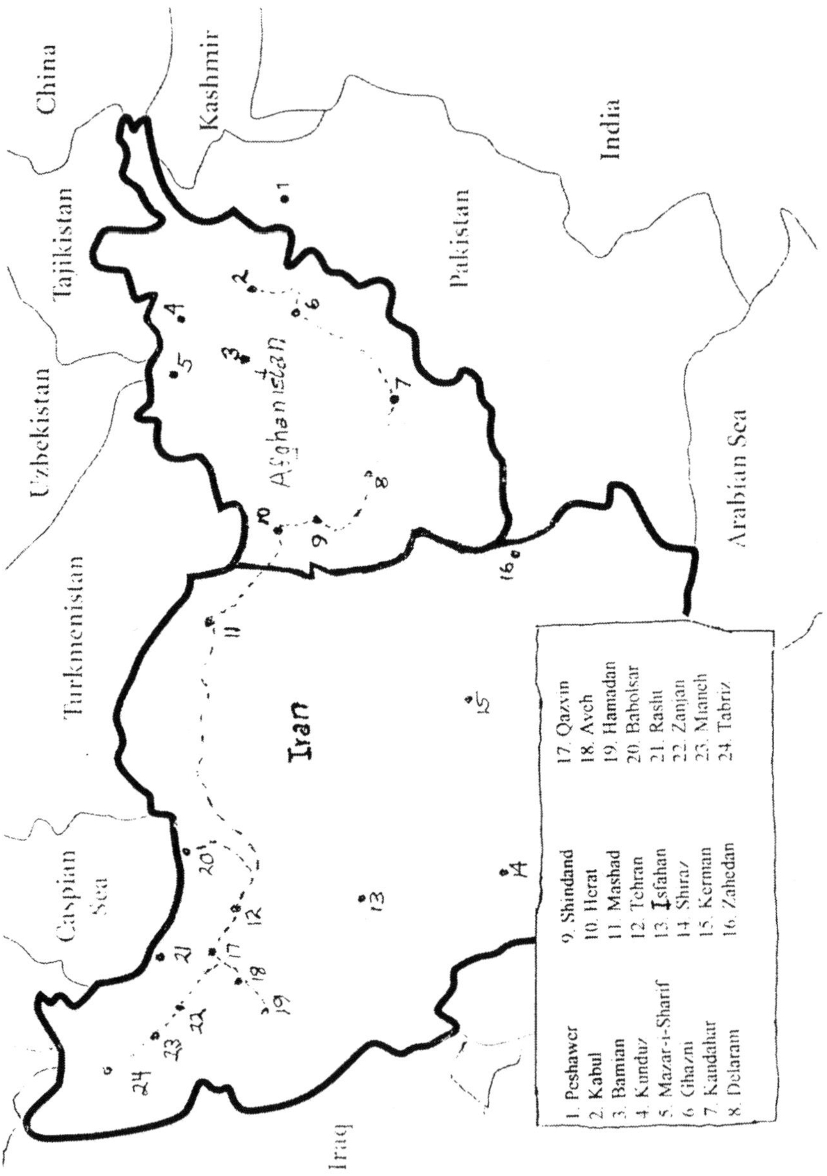
China
Kashmir
India
Tajikistan
Uzbekistan
Pakistan
Afghanistan
Turkmenistan
Arabian Sea
Caspian Sea
Iran
Iraq
1. Peshawer
2. Kabul
3. Bamian
4. Kunduz
5. Mazar-i-Sharif
6. Ghazni
7. Kandahar
8. Delaram
9. Shindand
10. Herat
11. Mashad
12. Tehran
13. Isfahan
14. Shiraz
15. Kerman
16. Zahedan
17. Qazvin
18. Aveh
19. Hamadan
20. Babolsar
21. Rasht
22. Zanjan
23. Mianeh
24. Tabriz

Introduction

Overleaf: *Wetherill and the bus that took us from Kabul to Herat.*

Chapter 1: Kabul to Tehran

Diary: May 16 – June 2, 1951; We Went to School in Tehran
Letters: May 23 and June 10, 1951; Holiday Letter: December 7, 1951

Wednesday, May 16, 1951.

It is all a delusion, but we feel that we are about to get off for Tehran. As far as we know Abdul Wakil Khan's[4] bus, commandeered in Kandahar, has not returned so it will be several days probably, before we can get started. This has been the funniest preparation for departure. With no definite date, my packing seemed aimless and interspersed with entertaining visitors, going out to lunches etc.

Osborne made a list for himself and each morning he started out on the same round for days and days, never seeming to get any business finished, but at least he finally got paid! He spent three solid weeks trying to get a passport for Nabi[5] and his family to go with us. Finally he was advised by the Foreign Minister and the Minister of Education to let the matter drop because Nabi might be beaten. Osborne did pick up a tip that it might be because he is Hazara.[6] One person offered to get him a passport but asked exorbitant baksheesh.[7] We shall probably never have two servants any pleasanter than Nabi and Kurban Ali.[8] They go out of their way to be helpful, are always cheerful and even suggested that they carry out our boxes to save paying a coolie!

4. Abdul Wakil Khan was our landlord and the owner of the bus. Our bus had been commandeered because of a flare up in the periodic border conflict between Afghanistan and Pakistan.

5. Nabi was our friend and servant for two years in Afghanistan, and he traveled with us on our ten-week winter trip to Iran. (*We Felt Their Kindliness...*, pp. 111-119, and the photo on p. 124) In the late 1970s Nabi helped another American family in Kabul and one of their children later wrote, "Nabi...made Afghanistan a home for us". I corresponded with her and we are certain it was the same man: Nabi was part of her family 25 years after he was part of ours. (Carla Power, "An American Childhood in Afghanistan," *Vogue*, December 2001, pp. 82, 84 & 86.)

6. In contrast with most Afghans, the Hazaras are Shiite and have Mongolian features. They are said to descend from garrison soldiers left by Genghis Khan.

7. Small bribes were a normal part of Afghan life.

8. Kurban Ali was a friend and servant, too. He was younger than Nabi and had not worked as a servant before he came to us. (*We Felt Their Kindliness...*, pp. 109-110, and the photo on p. 123)

During that time I guided the children thru another test[9] and packed about one box a day. It was the most leisurely packing I have ever done. Most all is packed except a suitcase for each of us, a food box and a rug bundle, which is a true Afghan solution to the packing problem.

Going thru *Gumruk* (Afghan Customs) was a breeze. With complete lists we opened only one trunk, the top only was looked at. They were most considerate and didn't disrupt my tight packing and now the trunks and boxes are wired and sealed so they don't have to be opened at the border. We can thank Mohammad Ali, translator at the U.S. Embassy for engineering it so easily.

We are now living a camping existence with our baggage and the *charpai*[10] that are already sold.

Saturday, May 19.

The Knudsen's have found a house and asked for Kurban Ali [to start working for them]. He wanted to stay with us to the bitter end and it would have been easier for us but we know how anxious you can become when you have been living with someone else and want to have your own home. Kurban Ali was back the next day to pick up some of his possessions and Friday morning, his day off, he was here to bring in our breakfast! He asked to come again today but Mrs. K. told him she was going to a party and would carry a message to us! We have tried to be kind to the servants and treat them as individuals and they have certainly responded with astonishing devotion.

At noon Osborne and Os had just returned from the usual round of post office etc. when Abdul Wakil arrived with a translator. As I was tying up Cavie[11] I heard the children shout, the men laugh and cries of "The bus is here." Sure enough, it is back in Kabul. Abdul Wakil suggested that we go out via Mezar-i-Sharif [in the north] instead of Kandahar – because of thievery and roughness down that way. We also suspect that the bus might be commandeered again. Since that is the

9. We used Calvert Correspondence School while in Kabul and loved it. I later did 8th grade with Calvert. (See their website, www.calverteducation.com)

10. *Charpai* are bed frames strung with rope.

11. Our dog's name was Cavie-Char, or Caversham IV.

one section of Afghanistan we have missed we agreed to go that way though we know it will be a mighty rugged trip and take a little longer. We don't, however, want to chance unpleasantness for the children and any more delay than we can help.

We have been threatening to get off for so long that when we went to the Military Attaché's party this afternoon everyone greeted us with, "I thought you had left!"[12] Wetherill and Os were allowed to go, too, and quite an impression they made. Os wandered around with the greatest dignity and sociability and was something of a sensation, having his picture taken with a tomato juice moustache and being dragged over by the French Ambassadress to meet the Court Minister (father-in-law of the Shah) to whom Os explained that he didn't think Tehran would be as interesting as Kabul because Tehran is too civilized. Madame told Osborne she almost split laughing. She corralled Wetherill to introduce her to dignitaries, too. And our hostess told Os that any time I got tired of him he could come back to live with her. Os sidled up to me and said, "I've heard two people say they thought I was the cutest thing they ever saw." He wrinkled his freckled nose and those big dark eyes twinkled – yes of course he enjoyed himself! Wetherill is shyer and didn't hear all the compliments about her poise and graciousness, but I never expected my ten-year-old daughter would greet half a dozen Ambassadors as special friends, and with no more confusion than in greeting a contemporary! They won't have that opportunity in Tehran, perhaps, but once having had it there is a backlog of assurance so they should be able to meet any new situation that may bob up. Maybe we weren't a pair of proud parents this day! Those children may turn out alright after all!!!

Osborne is already in bed – I wonder how many more nights we will sleep in Kabul? It will take us a bit longer, going the northern route, but with good luck we should be in Tehran in two weeks or a little more.

12. There were so few Americans in Kabul (my guess is about 60) that everyone was pretty much invited to everything.

Sunday, May 20.

After a day of anticipation we had a rude come down. When Osborne, Os and Abdul Wakil went to ask for additional coupons the Gas Monopoly told them not only might they not have more but perhaps they would take away those already issued! How discouraged we were then.

Monday, May 21.

Osborne and Os went back to find out the decision about gas – Farda [tomorrow, supposedly]. We all went to tea at the Iranian Embassy. Just a friendly family gathering on the back porch. His Excellency Mr. Ansari offered to help us about the gas if we couldn't manage for ourselves. He has sent us letters to Yusufabad and Mashhad and been most kind. Wetherill and Os had a wonderful time playing hide and seek in the big garden. Though Osborne and I came home at 6 PM the children by special invitation stayed until 7. Ezmari and Harold Popplestone[13] dropped in and Kurban Ali was just arriving when we got back. Poor Nabi spent most of the day collecting coal dust for himself from our storeroom and then made cookies until 10 o'clock. What a good young man he is!

Tuesday, May 22.

Osborne says we must have missed Tuesday but he arranged to leave tomorrow via Kandahar since we couldn't get gas for the north.[14] Amin stopped in, Ezmari and Harold had supper with us and we set off a firecracker to celebrate. Abdul Aziz, Ezmari's father, brought a letter to his relative, the Governor of Kandahar, and had tea with us. It was quite a celebration with our plastic plates, boxes for tables and Kurban Ali's charpai which he allowed us to keep to the last.

13. We were very close to Ezmari and his family. He was one of Osborne's students and traveled with us on the trip to Faizabad. Harold and Rosemary Popplestone were British friends. Rebecca and Osborne visited them in England in about 1970.

14. There were fewer towns on the northern route through Mazar-i-Sharif, and fewer opportunities to buy gasoline.

Wednesday, May 23.

What a day. Abdul Wakil was supposed to be at the house at 8 AM. At 9 Osborne went after him. At 10 his servant came to say he had gone to Paghman after the driver. Osborne and Wetherill took last minute things to the Bentons and while they were gone Abdul Wakil came to say he couldn't buy the gas, something was wrong with the coupons. Osborne took them around to numerous offices and had one more signature attached. We had lunch with Harold and said a fond farewell. Wetherill and I stopped to say goodbye to Barbara Percival and then waited while Osborne tried to catch up with Abdul Wakil to get the gas. The latter was at our house for final arrangements and payment. All attended to in good humor, but A. W. went out, Osborne stopped to receive money from Amin for our beds, and A. W. had disappeared.

After long searching Osborne and Ezmari found him. By then it was 6 PM so we sent word to Harold that we would accept his invitation for supper. When Osborne returned home at 7:40 PM with the bus (a rickety structure but pretty good engine) a policeman was with them! It seemed the epitome of our troubles: the cleaner[15] had no license! Amin took over, the children and I went to Harold's and Osborne came in soon after. Before dinner was over Ezmari came in to say Abdul Wakil wanted 500 Afs[16] more. Mohammad Jon, the "treasurer" who would be coming with us, said we would need it for camels! Osborne was furious.

Harold went home with us to see the bus and to hear what came of our arrangements. Amin was back at the house.

[The driver, Osborne, Ezmari and I went to get gasoline. We raced a city bus to the station with the last gas in Kabul, pulling up to the pump just in front of them and emptying it. That would only get us as far as Ghazni, 80 miles down the road, where we would have to buy more gas.]

Ezmari, Osborne and Harold went to Abdul Wakil's house, I put the children to bed on the wide bedroom window ledges with their mattresses and Amin kept me company until 10:30. A little after

15. The cleaner was an assistant driver.

16. Afs are Afghanis, the currency in Afghanistan. They were worth about four U.S. cents at the time.

eleven Osborne came in saying "We are going." The driver didn't have a passport but Osborne decided we should start and try to get the passport in Herat. Waiting here, even until tomorrow, might mean losing the gas coupons we have been allowed.

Nabi had stayed and he helped carry out the last 20 items. It was hard to leave Nabi, who was sweet and helpful to the very last, and we are going to regret more and more that we don't have him. I gave Cavie a last pat, roused the children, put on their sweaters, gave each a blanket and sent them out to the bus. A bed was made for them on top of trunks and boxes, just behind the one seat.[17] They were comfortable but so excited they couldn't go back to sleep. It was 12:05 AM when Osborne said Father Cresson's "Here we go-oo-o."

Thursday, May 24.

Ezmari rode with us to "Mary's corner" where he kissed the children, shook hands and kissed both Osborne's and my hands. As we rode down the main street, the children sang out "There is the Cinema, the hotel, Habibia etc."

How we did bump. Finally Osborne made a nook for himself at the children's feet and I stretched out on the hard seat. I had to put the *kosai*[18] over me because it was quite cold, a clear moonlit night. The hills looked lovely. At Shirabad the driver was sleepy so we stopped and all slept until dawn.

Drove to Ghazni where we had tea and *nawn*[19] at the hotel, took a few pictures and met a Morrison-Knudsen truck with a man who is

17. Intercity buses in Afghanistan usually had only a few seats with open space for boxes, luggage, mattresses, people, chickens and so on. It made it easy for travelers to visit with each other.

18. A *kosai* was a winter coat made of two layers of camel hair felt, long enough to hang to the shoe tops with equally long sleeves.

19. *Nawn* is whole wheat bread, baked in large thin platters with a rolled edge. It comes in many varieties. Here is Rebecca's easy recipe: take 6 tablespoons butter; 1½ cup finely chopped onions; ¾ cup warm water; 1 teaspoon salt; 2 to 2½ cups whole wheat flour; and ½ cup or more white flour (to make it stick together). Melt butter and cook onions until they become clear. Add water and flour and mix; it should be sticky. Make balls and flatten with rolling pin. Bake in dry frying pan or on hot griddle until flecked with brown on both sides. This makes 16 small tortilla shaped pieces of *nawn*.

going to take pictures of MK work in Afghanistan. Later met a German on his way to Kabul. He had been 12 days en route from Tehran, said the road was fine (or at least passable), and gave us the name of a nice French architect in Herat and an Austrian couple in Tehran whom he asked us to phone and tell that we had met him. He expected to get to Kabul by lunchtime but we told him it would be nearer supper for it was then almost 11 and takes five to six hours.

Had lunch in the bus – ham spread, *nawn*, powdered milk and orange crystals. Then everyone slept until 2:30, had tea and got off for the gas pumps at about 3:30. Got 40 gallons of gas with no trouble. The driver, cleaner and M'd Jon are warming up. Os was the first to crack the ice by his interest in all the bus activities. There are many nomads going north with babies and little camels riding, the grownups shooing the beasts off the road [as we came by]. In Ghazni many women in their dirty black and red outfits were shopping or selling camel milk *mawst* [yoghurt]. Their bracelets of copper or silver were tremendously wide. They often wore nose rings and hundreds of tiny pigtails.

Went as far as Danjan beyond Moqor where we arrived about 12 midnight. We took one passenger to Danjan who only wanted to go to Moqor. All the others thought it a good joke. Slept until 5, then started again. We rode up to what looked like a bad bump only to find that it was a bridge out! We would have had a serious accident if we had dumped over there and I agreed with the driver's fervent, "Allah". A little later we saw a bus half thru a bridge and then we <u>did</u> go cautiously. Ever after that the driver was rather perturbed and afraid of night driving.

Friday, May 25.

All day we bounced on toward Kandahar. The road did not seem quite so washboardy this time or are we perhaps inured? At one *chai-hawna*[20] we saw chained prisoners being walked from Kandahar to Kabul, a distance of 300 miles. One seated man was flushed with fever, a huddle of bones and tatters. He could walk only a few steps at

20. *Chai* was black tea with lots of sugar in the first cup, or glass, and little sugar in the last one. A *chai-hawna* was a teahouse where travelers and local people could rest, eat and socialize. These varied from simple restaurants to large rooms where people sat or lay on the floor on whatever they brought with them.

a time. We watched them go up the road we had traveled, knowing how many many miles it was before there was another habitation. [I was impressed when Osborne walked up to the seated prisoner and gave him food, and then took his picture, documenting his treatment.]

Saturday, May 26.

Spent the night in a serai[21] near Kandahar. In the morning M'd Jon went with us to see Amin's friend Yaiya, secretary to the Governor who had left the day before for Kabul. Yaiya felt as we did that M'd Jon was a slippery character and gave us a letter to the deputy Governor of Herat telling him M'd Jon had admitted to him that he was paid to go to Mashhad. M'd Jon doesn't want to go. Had tea (but skipped the cakes because they were thick with flies). On the way back Osborne suggested we stop at the hotel for a drink.[22] We had difficulty explaining this to M'd Jon who evidently had been well lectured by Yaiya about making haste.

A curly haired young boy recognized our name and explained he is a cousin of our friend, Moussa. He introduced us to Sardar Kabir, one of 68 sons of Habibullah Khan, Shah of Afghanistan in the early 1900s. Mrs. Kabir is a Tarzi (a royal family). They are parents of Gulalai who translated for Pearl Campbell in Kabul. We had a pleasant visit.

[I remember well the intense and friendly gaze of Sardar Kabir as he studied me. We were each unusual in the other's experience. This chance encounter later had a great effect on the outcome of our journey.]

M'd Jon and driver were angry about the delay. Got off at 6 o'clock and found that contrary to information given us, none of the three men had ever been to Herat. At Gereshk I remembered the first turn but was in doubt at the next, outside town. Picked up three passengers, a mullah and companions. The children slept, and Osborne and I a bit also. Stopped for remainder of night because driver was afraid of getting lost.

21. A compound where travelers rest, or a bus terminal.

22. We were snowbound for three weeks in this hotel during our ten week trip through Afghanastan and Iran the year before. (See *We Felt Their Kindliness . . .*, Chapter 27: Winter Journey.)

Sunday, May 27.

Next morning we went on, making many stops to tinker with the engine all these days. Changed tires twice. Crossed a river, engine stalled, everyone swam and I went in knee deep. On to Delaram for rest and tea, then a fine swim in my dress. Children remembered quite a bit and could float after a few tries. Started off happily, everyone friendly. Crossed two difficult narrow places – one especially bad. Three Morrison Knudson trucks helped out. At dusk found the truck's lights wouldn't work.

Osborne periodically hammered nails back into our boxes and Os screwed down the screws that were jounced loose but there wasn't anything that we could do about the sand that sifted in everywhere.

Stopped for *chai* after starting again. Then M'd Jon came begging to spend the remainder of night – it was 11. We had gone about as far as two hours' worth of driving.

Monday, May 28.

Started at 5 AM, drove one hour and then waited 1½ hours at a serai for tea. M'd Jon had his and left us waiting – mean individual. To Farah by 9 AM. Then M'd Jon said he wanted more tea, we said "No, go on." He said he had to get a light bulb. After 1½ hrs waiting he said it was too hot. We think he wanted to wait to collect more passengers. Osborne insisted upon going on, not realizing it was so far and so hot to the next serai. Abdul Wakil had said we could travel by day after Farah, but it was terribly hot and in spots there was no water.

Then a piston rod broke ten minutes from Shindand. It was patched enough to arrive. [The cleaner rode on the fender using his feet to hold a board against the hole in the engine block. On hills, the passengers had to get out and walk. Rebecca dug out a multicolored roll of Lifesaver candies she had been saving and gave us each one for energy.]

M'd Jon claimed we would have to pay for a new engine. Osborne knew heat wouldn't make a piston break. No one in the town spoke English or French. The cleaner was friendly but cautious because he had to get on with M'd Jon. The driver was sad but did not blame us.

I think he was glad to get out of going into a strange country – strange roads in his own country were too much for him.

[The situation was becoming desperate. We were left with a truck load but no truck because of what M'd Jon said was an act of God. Worse, there were no banks in Herat and we had very little cash since taking funds out of Afghanistan was prohibited except by permission tediously obtained in Kabul.]

Fortunately, Sardar Kabir, whom we met in Kandahar, was on a mail bus which arrived just then. He arranged to have Hakim, the local Governor, get a truck for us. Kabir decided M'd Jon was a complete scoundrel and said to have him come with us to Herat where he would deal with him "like a rat."

Tuesday, May 29.

Got up to see Kabir and Madam off. Then trouble began. M'd Jon tried to pay us off and not go to Herat, realizing probably that Osborne and Kabir were on the trail of his misuse of gas coupons. My Farsi is a little quicker than Osborne's so M'd Jon dragged me into it and the manager of the hotel tried to help him out – not pushing too much to get in bad with Kabir but trying to see if we would hurry off on our own. We said no. M'd Jon must stay with us, or we would not go to Herat. Governor Hakim came in and arranged for us to leave with M'd Jon at 3 PM. Kabir phoned back from Herat to be sure we were getting off. A rather dejected M'd Jon made one last attempt to abandon us but we stood pat and we shall see what he will try next. Up to the very last he was lying and devious.

Finally, at 6 PM we got off in a lorry [a truck] – dusty, windy, and cold by turns. Ten other passengers were pleasant companions. The cleaner was a talkative, friendly boy who complained about the discomforts more than we did. Osborne and the children slept but I stayed awake watching the rising mountains clouded in dust. The road was washed out in many places and the detours were rocky but we made good time for change. We moved fast and got to Herat in 3½ hours.

At the city gate the soldier said he was expecting us and sent us on thru. The other passengers got out and we stopped at a *chai-hawna* that was a picture. A black hole in the wall with a narrow rack for teapots on which a flickering light was cast by a single candle stuck to the top shelf. The cleaner brought a lantern, which he tied to the top of the lorry, and a tray of glasses for tea and some sugar lumps. The *nawn* was thin with blisters all over it – tasty but not as rich as Kabul's *nawn.* He didn't let us pay for it, just why I'll never know unless M'd Jon was trying to get in our good graces.

Arrived at the hotel at 9:30 or 10 PM. Osborne wouldn't unload the truck until speaking to Kabir who had gone out for dinner so the four of us stretched out on our mattresses with the wind tossing the pine trees over our heads. After a while a car brought the Kabirs and Osborne spoke to Sardar. He told a soldier to guard our things well and we all went into the hotel to sleep – the first time in a week in a real bed. It felt strange!

Wednesday, May 30.

A bit before eight there was a knock and breakfast call. Osborne had it brought to our room, but we had not finished when negotiations for paying rascally M'd Jon started.

[Sardar Kabir had arranged for a court hearing. Osborne and I waited outside the meeting room as a parade of severe looking mullahs came down the hall and swept into the room, barely glancing at us. Soon someone opened the door and told Osborne to come in.]

It took three hours of talk, much of it spent contradicting what M'd Jon said. He was the worst bold-faced liar I've ever met. He had evidently done something with the gas coupons but no one seemed interested in prying into that. The "Principal in Charge of Service to Foreigners" who was handling the dealings decided that M'd Jon should return 900 Afs to us – Osborne was willing to pay the rest because of the expense Abdul Wakil was going to have.

In the afternoon we went to see the Iranian Consul. We had letters from Amin and another friend for him. He gave us tea, cucumbers, apricots and green plums. His little daughter, aged two, came in. We also had a very pleasant chat with the English teacher who had translated for the business deal. Saw Mr. Barrois, a French architect, and visited with Mr. and Mrs. Kabir. Mosquitoes bit us to bits in the night.

Thursday, May 31.

The children were out meeting people the first thing in the morning, while I washed out some sox, jeans, etc. The trip was so hot and dusty our clothes didn't hold out well. Osborne and the children met Richard and Elizabeth Ettinghausen from Freer Gallery in Washington.[23] He was a German refugee and she from Austria. They had just come from Mashhad where the Cochrans[24] told them of us. They are looking for Islamic Art. Herat was once the capital of Iran and a center of artistic development. Mr. E. has not been able to find a single piece of art from that time.

We ate pilau at noon in the dining room. In the afternoon Mr. and Mme. Barrois, Mr. and Mrs. Ettinghausen and four Cressons went to see the old mosque ruins in two *gawdies* [two-wheeled horse-drawn carriages used as taxis in Afghanistan]. It dated in the early 1400s. The old, broken towers must have been beautiful when completely faced with tile. The texture of the tile was fine – turquoise blue, royal blue with a little tan, black and green. The inside of the mosque was stucco painted to resemble tile which used to be done. It had suffered with the passage of time. The mosque was built by Gawhar Shad, a daughter-in-law of Tamerlane and now has a mullah's school in a new compound with a tiny new mosque of baked yellow brick.

All of us toured the bazaars where we saw little of interest. Things were even cruder than in Kabul though there were many quaint shops. Back in the hotel we had tea and *nawn* with smoked shad, milk and cookies from our food box for supper. Saw the hotel museum and a large picture of Habibullah, father of Sardar Kabir. Mosquitoes are bad. Wetherill and I are bitten all over. Taking Aralen in hopes of avoiding malaria. [Osborne, Wetherill and Os had malaria the year before.]

[Always scribbling under the pressure of time, Rebecca sometimes wrote just a few words about what was a complex and intriguing event. The Herat hotel used to be a palace and I enjoyed exploring it.

23. Dr. Richard Ettinghausen, an expert on Islamic art, was head curator of the Freer Gallery of Art in Washington DC.

24. Joseph and Bernice Cochran were missionaries in Mashhad and old friends of Rebecca whose father, Thomas Berry Shannon, had been a Presbyterian minister. Unfortunately, she barely knew her father since he died when she was two-years-old.

One day, up a spiral staircase in a small tower, I found a door locked with a seal. Mother and Dad told Sardar Kabir and he got the manager who had someone break the lock. We all crowded in, mouths agape: the small room was stuffed with colorful furnishings and art objects. On the wall was a large portrait of an impressive gentleman who Sardar Kabir, speaking reverently, said was his father, Habibullah Khan. He was a moderate reformer assassinated in 1919 by an Indian spy hired by Britain. The spy was later arrested when the same people paid him to try to kill Kemal Ataturk, the first president of modern Turkey.]

Friday, June 1.

Took a *gawdie* down to the new mosque – several hundred years old! It is tile-faced and handsome with parts that have been repaired in inferior design. Large, splotchy bold colors instead of many beautifully blended small designs. We wandered back thru the old city to the bazaar where we bought a little hat which both Wetherill and I can wear. After pilau I washed clothes. Osborne and the children played games and then I read *Pilgrim Kate* to them.

At six we joined the Ettinghausens, Barrois, two French ladies and rode out to a beautiful hill spot overlooking the Herat plain. Men were swimming in a large pool. The "Principal in Charge of Service to Foreigners" came and was most gracious. Tables were set with flat pan-fried puff cakes. There were green almonds and tea. Mrs. E. took pictures after the arrival of the Deputy Governor, for whom the tea was given by the Ettinghausens. Then we had ice cream. Os was worried about undulant fever and we did cross our fingers hoping the milk had been boiled. When we got back to the hotel we all took Enterovioform.[25] Sardar Kabir brought in a desert plume blossom for me when he returned from a day long visit to a friend up near the Iranian border.

Saturday, June 2.

Osborne checked our passport at the Iranian Consulate. We

25. This is Rebecca desperately trying to keep her family healthy in an environment in which any sip of untreated water could cause life-threatening dysentery. We only drank boiled water, sometimes upsetting waiters when we insisted they rinse the cups or glasses with hot tea.

packed in preparation for departure this afternoon. This stay in Herat has been a restful interlude after the rugged days en route.

Now, more trouble. We were promised transport to Yusufabad [in Iran] on the mail bus, but one hour before it left they bounced us off. Sardar Kabir thinks there is collusion between the officials to get more money. They are charging 1000 Afs just to take us to Yusufabad. It's another gouge, for we had to hire a whole bus. It's too bad to leave with such bitter final experiences.

Sunday, June 3.

The merchant who was so friendly in Mashhad on our trip last year entertained us royally for dinner the day we left. The little old customs man at Islam Kala was nice and cleared our baggage with no trouble.

Monday, June 4 – Thursday, June 7.

At Yusufabad we were treated well. Ambassador Ansari's letter helped, and the fact that the visiting Customs Inspector was an American College graduate. They gave us lunch and arranged for our transport to Mashhad.

We arrived in Mashhad on Tuesday at 6 AM. Joe and Bernice Cochran were almost ready for their breakfast on the porch with two visitors when the <u>dirtiest</u> Cressons walked in on them. Had a lovely visit with them and a pleasant dinner the second night with Frank and Jean Woodward. Such a cordial welcome from all and an early start on Thursday for Tehran. Most friendly companions on a comfortable bus but we sat up all night and stopped for only a few one-hour rest periods. Went thru a blinding dust storm and so were again frightfully dirty when we arrived in Tehran.

[It had taken us 16 days to go 1415 miles, the distance from Boston to Minneapolis.]

Friday, June 8 – Saturday, June 9.

Tehran has sparkling fountains at some of its street intersections. They looked unbelievably cool and refreshing as we lumbered into town with all our possessions. The journey had been long, hot, and dusty – the kind that makes you wonder why you ever thought of doing it. Tehran seemed like a world apart.

We got in about 2:30 in the afternoon and Osborne went on a 5-minute walk to the Mission. John Elder[26] came to show the bus driver where to take our baggage – to the old hospital grounds where Community School is going to move this summer. It is one or two miles from Central Compound which is a beautiful tree-grown campus with an extensive building and several houses.[27]

It was like coming home to arrive in Tehran where we had visited 1½ years ago. The people of the mission gave us a royal welcome. And it was the school's Commencement Day! We were rushed to a tea party within two hours of our arrival and much to our surprise we ended our first day, as members of a mission, by dancing at a final school dance! There was a double birthday party the next night where we enjoyed a grand sing. They were so glad to have a new tenor and wished I were an alto. So do I.

The house we are to have is now occupied, so we will be in an apartment for a few weeks and eat around with others. We are staying this weekend with Tom and Frankie Fisher, so Osborne can soak up as much information as possible. [Mr. Fisher was the departing school principal.]

One of the best bits of news we heard that first day is that a principal has been found so that Osborne can concentrate on the business management and upper school math classes. He didn't look forward to schedule planning and teacher placement in addition to the task of supervising needed repairs and construction. Osborne will have to carry the load until September when the new Mr. and Mrs. Irvine[28] will arrive. So far I don't know what I shall be doing.

26. John and Ruth Elder were leaders of the Presbyterian mission community in Iran. We stayed in their home until our housing was arranged. Their son, David, who grew up in Tehran, later worked for the American Friends Service Committee in Philadelphia and helped me edit and publicize *We Felt Their Kindliness: An American Family's Afghan Odyssey 1949-1953.*

27. Buildings in Iran were often in compounds, surrounded by high walls. The Presbyterian Mission in Tehran had an old compound with school, church and homes, and a new compound with a hospital soon to be converted to a school and more homes. There were gardens and playgrounds in both compounds.

28. Richard Irvine, the school principal, and Mary Ann Irvine, the music teacher and choir director, lived in the house next door to us in the new compound.

The youngsters are interested in square dancing and will have scouts and dramatics and many activities. It is going to be a busy life. Osborne is working already and is swamped, or will be.

So our new experience has begun. Friendly and kindly everyone has been. If the problems seem tremendous, we know that in a day and a half we haven't comprehended them all!!

This is the bus that took us from Kabul to Herat (barely). Wetherill is at the door, Os' bicycle visible on the roof. Nails bounced out of boxes and sand sifted into the very center of trunks.

The bus stopped in an Afghan village to pick up passengers. Some are already on the roof.

Donkeys and their drivers waiting for a job.

We met prisoners being walked from Kandahar to Kabul. Osborne took food to the seated man who looked very ill.

A crowd on a very old bridge.

Below: *The tomb of Goharshad in Herat. She married a son of Tamerlane, became de facto ruler of the empire, and led a cultural renaissance.*

The Great Mosque of Herat has had recent renovations. Wetherill and Os are in left foreground.

The bus we hired in Herat, about to cross from Afghanistan into Iran.

Tehran

Overleaf: A view of Tehran.

Chapter 2: The City

Letters: June 29, 1951 and June 24, 1952
Diary: Dec. 21, 1950; We Went to School in Tehran

The major part of Tehran is quite modern with baked brick buildings, the apartment houses and streets running at mathematical right angles. The main avenues are wide and paved. The extremely narrow *kuchehs* (alleys) are often hard surfaced, too. In south Tehran there are neighborhoods where people live in caves and broken-down mud hovels, ignorant and poor.

Taxi drivers have all the dash and daring of tribesmen, schooling back and forth, passing cars on the right at corners, skimming the coattails of pedestrians who pay little attention to traffic signals, and miraculously avoiding bicyclists who obey no traffic laws whatsoever. Having come to Tehran from Afghanistan where taxies are two-wheeled carts drawn by broken down horses, I found the pace of Tehran alarmingly fast at first.

When one learns to accept Tehran traffic with detachment and to look above the maelstrom, one sees domes and minarets and blue-tiled doorways. However there is no architecture as astoundingly lovely as some that is found in Isfahan which was Iran's capital during one of the country's greatest artistic periods. Nor does Tehran have the grandeur of the city of shrines, Mashhad.

In many ways there seems little that is different from what you all see in your own hometowns – there are no street cars or subways but many buses; the taxies are mostly small European cars (with a few horse-drawn *droshkies* that look something like "Victorias"); people wear European clothes, and if there are more swarthy skins, black eyes and aquiline features than you see some places, it is something to which we have become accustomed.

We found a few signs of the old East in Tehran. *Farda*, which means tomorrow, is even more vague than the proverbial mañana, while *farda inshallah* (tomorrow, God willing) is very likely never to happen at all. It is accepted as a polite way of saying that you wish you might but you don't believe you will.

Another old tradition is begging. The accomplished school

of professional mendicants has been suppressed but we do see some pathetic specimens in tatters. I fear to give money for then you are spotted and have a permanent following. On one bus trip we stopped at a village and we got out for tea and *nawn* but the beggars were so persistent that we came back to the bus and ate cookies instead. The driver hopped out and gave some beggars a few coins. Hordes more pushed up begging. Then an army officer clambered out to buy something. After he finished his purchase, he gave a brother officer who was standing there some money for the beggars.

On rare occasions in Tehran we still see camels file past the Parliament building in gawky superciliousness. Donkeys push up onto the sidewalks to deliver their burdens of vegetables or charcoal, flocks of turkeys are driven down the main street in the fall and sometimes bewildered sheep scurry along toward the butcher.

Tehran's streets are alive with venders. During summer's heat men with porous earthen jugs, a glass, and a bit of ice sell cooling drinks on the streets. Others roast ears of corn over charcoal. In winter, itinerants offer steaming slices of beetroot and kabobs. Many cry their wares in a melodious, minor key patter. The Popsicle man who came by our street was called the "Alaska man," and a company dispenses yogurt, called *mawst*, in pint sized earthenware jars with labels showing a costumed mouse and the product name – "Miki Mawst"!

Chapter 3: Shopping

Diary: Dec. 21, 1950; Letters: June 29, 1951 and June 24, 1952
The House at 51 Howellville Road; We Went to School in Tehran

Yeksabet[29], our cook, did most of our shopping. I tried to persuade her to buy food for several days at a time, but the habit of daily marketing was too deeply ingrained, and she disliked hiring a porter. Each morning she took her basket and for several hours toured the scattered food shops. Here she would find the vegetable dealer; blocks away would be neatly tiled butcher stalls, their freshly killed beef and lamb hanging in the warm sunshine. Much farther on would be sellers of flour; of potatoes or rice; of melons – especially Persian melons of unforgettable flavor; of shiny red pomegranates and occasionally oranges and bananas; of fresh dates, unpackaged and full of sticks, but more tasty than any I have come across elsewhere; of walnuts, almonds, and pistachios, and squash and watermelon seeds.

Shopping expeditions sometimes carried us to the city's old section, to the huge Old Bazaar, which stretches for blocks in every direction under a great vaulting of brick. There, from narrow, shadowy stalls, come the hammer beats of brass and copper smiths and the glow of their tiny forges. In countless other stalls shoemakers cobble, tailors ply their needles, carpenters work in wood. Artisans of every type abound, most of them working entirely by hand.

When shopping for dress materials I went to the Old Bazaar with Iranian friends. There were bolts and bolts of material in bewildering quantities and varying widths. Each merchant has a small selection and if you do not find just what you want or enough of what you choose, he is quite willing to borrow from a neighbor. His neighbor is just as likely to try to entice you away with some other choices!

You can buy almost any conceivable object in the Old Bazaar, threading the cobbled aisles, avoiding ladened donkeys, and porters carrying equally large loads, and boys selling notions – persistent rascals who look so dejected it takes a hard, or case-hardened heart to

29. Yeksabet was named Elizabeth in Armenian.

resist their pleas. Our *giveh,*[30] needles, bobby pins, brass samovar and a rug all came from the Old Bazaar.

Along the street called Naderi there are western type stores where prices are often fixed. It is a little confusing at first to know whether or not a merchant really means it when he says that his prices are *feex.* After numerous trials and about as many errors one begins to find out.

Shopkeepers occasionally put the price higher if you bought in quantity, with the fascinating eastern logic that the man who wishes to buy large quantities can, presumably, afford to pay more!

For better bargaining I usually took one of the children with me. Wetherill smiled and then looked sad when the quoted price was too high. Os' technique was quite different. When he was told a high price he grinned cheerfully at the merchant, clucked his tongue and teasingly told the man he was a *shatun* (little devil). Both systems worked fairly well, though Os' American accent and Wetherill's blue eyes clearly identified them as foreigners and therefore likely prospects for high prices.

I have never known a city with so many silver shops. How any merchant makes a living is beyond my understanding of Iranian economics. In most shops silver is sold by weight and the number of man-hours that have gone into the articles receives no consideration. There are three popular types of silver work, Zanjan work is filigree, Tabriz has geometric borders and that of Isfahan, completely engraved with flowers, birds, curlicues and leaves.

The best workmanship is the engraved work that was done years ago though very fine designs can be found in hammer and chisel work. We learned to distinguish between the hammer and chisel work on brass and designs that had been stamped.

I discovered that the shops in Tehran were taking ancient trays and burnishing off the *sefid,* a white, pewter-like overlay put on all Muslim copperware according to instructions in the Koran. After removing the *sefid,* new scenes from Persian poetry were etched on the plain band that traditionally ran around between a center medallion and a narrow border.

30. Iranian sandals with woven tops made of fine knots of string and leather soles.

"Americans like old things and they like Persian miniature type designs – so we give them both," a merchant told me candidly. I ran my fingers across designs and usually avoided articles that had sharp new cuts. The old plain things had beauty enough of their own and I wished the merchants would leave them that way.

I often stopped to browse among Daveed's beautiful objects when I went to the USIE[31] library near his store. I frankly told him that I came only to look because he set his prices too high for me to buy anything. He appreciated my interest if not my attitude and took time to tell me about ancient ornaments and utensils. One evening Osborne and I left the library and found Daveed waiting for us beside the door of his shop. He called to us that he had something special to show. There in his shop were three ancient trays in all their simplicity. I drooled over them and urged Daveed to sell them just as they were. He asked which I liked best, but I reminded him that I never bought anything in his shop. He said, "Buy this at any price that you want to pay. I will accept whatever you offer." He made a good deal because we paid him an honest price, more than he expected! The tray has the words of the first verse of the Koran in the center. Other words on the outside border no one has been able to translate. Was the artist illiterate?

Buying rugs for our house was quite taxing. First a dealer came to the house and any rug that he could persuade us to keep for a few days stayed with us until we were thoroughly convinced that it was not what we wanted. The dealer finally agreed with us that he didn't seem to have what we required.

Our trouble was that we knew that a fine close weave might mean a good rug. Unfortunately, we also knew that the edges should be straight, the rug should not hump along the floor and that the color should not come off if you spit and rubbed with a hankie.

"I'm going to stop looking at the backs and choose a rug that I like from the front," Osborne declared after months of ruglessness. Forthwith we acquired rugs!

31. The United States International Information and Education Exchange (USIE) was a U.S. State Department program. It later became the United States Information Agency (USIA).

The first came from the government rug store where prices are definitely *feex.* It is 5 feet × 7 feet with a border of green which is most unusual. There is dark blue, cream and terracotta in the border and center medallion. Around the medallion the background is cream with gold outlined gray floral designs and swirls in deep turquoise, green, blue and terracotta. It is not a very fine weave but has such rich and pleasing colors that we are very well satisfied.

The second rug was more laboriously acquired in a typically Eastern way. We went with a friend to see her distant relative who is a rug exporter. He was not in his office the first day so that we went back another day. When we located him he telephoned to a friend in the Old Bazaar and we went down to see <u>him</u>. The dealer had coolies turn over rug after rug, straight thru a large pile.

We found two that looked like possibilities. They were pulled out and put on top. We walked on them and examined them. The merchant insisted that we wait to make a decision until the next day when he would have a new shipment opened, so again we waited. After finally making our decision we waited some more – until our friend's relative could go to inspect our choice and decide whether the price was fair.

This rug is about 12 feet × 14 feet with a dusty rose background which is most unusual but good for our living room which is fairly dark due to much greenery and a wide porch outside its windows. The design is not one you see in exported rugs but rather a tribal type such as women have woven for years for their own use. It has five or six varieties of deer, flowers and birds which makes a very nice, unobtrusive pattern. I was pleased when we went to an Iranian birthday party and saw a gorgeous, finely woven carpet with a quite similar design!

So we finally have some rugs and I think they will be very satisfactory to live with. One of the old-time missionaries told me that even though they are not exceptionally fine rugs they are good ones and our great-grandchildren would still be using them!! Funny to think of!

Our Household

Overleaf: *Rebecca and Osborne in their living room in Tehran.*

Yeksabet, whose wide experience and dedication kept our home functioning smoothly (as much as possible).

The milkman with Yeksabet beside our home. He asked Osborne to put off the picture for a day so he could dress up.

Batool with her mother and Mariam, Mina and Mehri who insisted on being in the picture, too. Batool was cheerful and hardworking and we enjoyed her company.

Yeksabet and Batool in front of our first home in Tehran, in the Presbyterian Mission's Central Compound.

After church in the Central Compound in Tehran. Rebecca is on the left, with Anne, Margie and Wetherill in the center.

The Community school chorus, led by Mary Ann Irvine, with Anne, 2nd from the left, then Os beside her. Margie is in the center wearing plaid, and Wetherill on the right.

A picnic during a long hike. From the right are Osborne, Os, Wetherill (only her knees!), Rebecca, Margie and Anne.

Anne Wild in the Central Compound in Tehran.

Margie Frame on the Community School playground.

Anne and Margie, posing like statues in the New Compound in Tehran.

Wetherill is carrying Margie toward the front door of our first home in the Mission's Central Compound. Os is walking up while Rebecca waits in the walkway. Community School students were playing ball in front of the house.

On an outing, Os, Margie, Wetherill and Margie's mother, Adelaide Hoffman, take a break on a stone wall.

Wetherill on the front steps of our second home, dressed up for her first formal party.

Wetherill happily posing for her proud Dad.

Osborne and Wetherill in the Central Compound.

Os on the playground in the New Compound. It was used for soccer, baseball, track and school celebrations.

Rebecca and Osborne in our living room. You can see a portrait of Saqao, our watercarrier in Kabul, and the old clock that followed us half way around the world and still worked. The old Persian oil lamp beside Osborne was converted to electricity and now sits beside my bed in Iowa City.

Rebecca and Osborne on the steps of our first home, in Central Compound.

Chapter 4: Yeksabet and Batool

[Two women worked for us from almost our first to our last day in Iran. They were wise and hardworking and they enjoyed helping us learn about their country.]

We Went to School in Tehran
Letters: November 12, 1951 and March 25, 1952

Yeksabet, a woman of Armenian extraction, was about 48. Both of her children had been educated in an American mission school. Keeping her accounts was a complicated routine. Her notes were in Armenian script, she told them to me in Farsi and I wrote them down in English!

Yeksabet did the cooking and practically all the shopping, even helping the children with their Christmas buying and choosing wool for sweaters and sox. All Os' peculiar requirements from the ducks to a giant-sized magnet, Yeksabet attended to with a willing *chashm* ["upon my eye," like "your word is my command"].

When she needed more money for the household she modestly asked for *kam-i-pul* (a little money). If pressed for an exact amount she would admit to wanting anything from 25 Rials (50¢) to 1000 Rials, but it was always *kam* in the first mention.

Batool, at 40, had a 25-year-old son (Hassan). She did the cleaning and the laundry, and petted the girls and laughed at Os' clowning with the best good humor. Like Yeksabet, Batool was a Christian although all her family were Muslims.

One day in November when the chrysanthemums were pretty in the garden, Batool picked a bouquet of yellow and deep rusty maroon ones which she put in a turquoise blue Afghan bowl in the study. She realized how much I enjoy flowers and noticed that I hadn't had time to pick them recently.

The differences in our two servants' habits and furnishings are indicative of the various cultures and customs within Iran. [They lived near us in the school compound.] Yeksabet's apartment had chairs, tables and beds while, when we first knew her, Batool's elderly mother kept her house in the old Iranian style folding away the sleeping pads each morning and serving meals on a cloth on the floor. By the time we left she had adopted the use of chairs and tables.

Os enjoyed taking his Farsi lesson to Batool's house in winter. A pot of charcoal was set under a low table and covered with a quilt. The family sat on the floor with bolsters at their backs, the quilt drawn over their knees and their toes as close to the small fire as they felt convenient. Os liked to snuggle in with little Mariam close by to prompt him as he read his Farsi. I suspect that Grandmother sometimes fed him candies or pistachios.

[Gathering with friends under the quilt in Batool's home is one of my fondest memories of Iran. Large trays heaped with food were sometimes placed in the center from which we served our own plates and then, to my delight, we ate with our fingers. There was a lot of warmth in that room.]

Batool invited us to tea one *No Ruz.* I moaned before going that I was too tired to try to carry on a conversation in Farsi and the children thought it quite an obligation, too, but all three of us came home happy and stimulated by the friendliness and goodwill. There were Batool, her mother, a sister who does our dressmaking, and another sister's little daughter whom Batool is rearing. We were the only guests. Though she provided chairs we chose to sit on the floor and had spread before us numerous dishes of nuts, candies, cookies and squash seeds. Little Mariam insisted that perfume be sprinkled on our hands, which we were directed to rub on our hair. As at all Iranian social affairs, we drank cup after cup of tea. Wetherill and I read a few pages of Mariam's Farsi first reader and Os found that he could add with Farsi numerals. It was a particularly friendly and pleasant party even though the only language we could use was our faulty Farsi.

The following day Batool had a large party for her family and friends. When I suggested that she might bake cookies in our kitchen she shyly told me that her friends would feel that she did not compliment them if she served home cooked sweets! Well she knew that I never "complimented" my friends but always served cookies from our own kitchen! This is a common feeling – the girls who planned the school teacher and parent teas felt the same way. "Boughten" things are better than homemade – isn't that too bad.

Batool also could never understand my love of plain, old things. She chuckled over my selections, saying, "My mother threw that away 20 years ago!"

Yeksabet did not want a holiday during New Year's but chose to have Easter week which is the Armenian time for paying and receiving visits. We dropped in at many friends' homes during Easter and drank innumerable cups of tea and the children collected colored eggs at each house we visited.

Iranian servants freely voice their opinions. Ours were no exception. In our home a teakettle of water was always kept on the stove to add moisture to the air and we thought it most convenient for a cup of coffee before retiring. Batool didn't approve of coffee at night so for a long time I made a tour of the house each evening to assemble the coffee tray. The milk was in the kitchen, powdered coffee in the study and cups in the dining room. I had to forgive Batool and merely chuckle at my nightly travels for she kept the house immaculate in spite of four children.

When Batool had her holiday, Yeksabet would sometimes indulge me and set the coffee tray before she left, after dinner, but in other ways she was very strict with us. If we asked for food that was out of season or expensive Yeksabet was apt to have a sudden loss of memory.

One day we planned a rather large tea party and both servants disapproved when I suggested caviar sandwiches. I insisted that I wanted them and then tore off to my scheduled duties in the library, a teachers' meeting, a scout meeting, a Farsi lesson and by the time I got home for tea there was only a moment to glance at the arrangements that our faithful servants had made. I discovered the caviar sandwiches – if they could be called such. There was bread and butter and when you looked closely you found a precious few dark specks of caviar smeared across the buttery surface. My vision of mounds of salty richness was certainly flattened out.

But when five of us went to bed with bad cases of flu Yeksabet and Batool devotedly took turns staying all night. In the dark hours a quiet figure rose from her bed in the hall and carried medicines from room to room. Never in all the days and nights of their care were the medicines more than five minutes off schedule. (Wetherill kept track.)

I couldn't have managed my busy program without our two excellent helpers.

Chapter 5: Margie and Anne

[We spent almost two months living in Ruth and John Elder's home in the Central Compound. They made us feel wonderfully welcome, but it was exciting to move into our own home nearby. It was currently occupied by the missionaries Mark and Ruth Irwin, not to be confused with Richard and Mary Ann Irvine.]

Letter: July 22, 1951

It has now been decided that we will move into the Irwin's house, next door to the Elder's house, and since it is a big house, take Margie Frame[32] who will be in 5th Grade with Os and Anne Wild,[33] an English child who will be in my 3rd Grade, as boarders. Os is afraid that he is going to be awfully henpecked but we shall have four boys for lunches as well! Seems we are going to have a large family, at least temporarily.

Hope to get settled this week, though the Irwins probably won't move out completely, for on Wednesday they are due to go to the "Garden" in the hill suburb of Shemiran where Bill Miller is conducting conferences. (Another change. Probably move about the 30th). So – at long last we have a place to think of as home. There are four bedrooms and two dressing-rooms upstairs; large living-room, study, den and dining-room downstairs. The den will be Os' special entertainment room and the girls can use their more spacious bedrooms. Osborne will have a study and I room in our bedroom. In winter we will probably

32. Margaret Adelaide Frame, "Margie" with a hard "g", was the daughter of two medical missionaries working in Resht, Iran, and the step-daughter of a third. Her mother and father were Adelaide Kibbe Frame and John Davidson Frame, Sr., and her step-father was Rolla Edwards Hoffman. These three dedicated doctors worked in Iran for a total of 112 years. They lived in Resht, on the Caspian Sea, but Margie was born in the hospital we were using as a school. She could even visit the room in which she took her first breath! Margie published her mother's story in *Passage to Persia: Writings of an American doctor during her life in Iran,* 1929-1957. UK: Summertime Pub., 2014.

33. Catherine Anne Wild was the daughter of Mary Wild, a teacher, and Peter Wild, a surgeon. They were Anglicans working for the Church Missionary Society in Kerman (where Anne was born), Isfahan and Shiraz from 1942 to 1972. Happily, Wetherill and I are still in touch with Margie and Anne.

heat only dining-room and den. The Irvines (principal of Community School) are expected in 8 days. They will take our places at the Elder's until their boxes arrive.

Holiday Letter: December 7, 1951

Margie Frame is Os' "twin" for she has wide apart brown eyes, is in fifth grade, too, and only six weeks younger than Os. Anne Wild is eight, a third grader who is almost as tall as Os and the quick, energetic type which makes her a special pal of our lad. She helps him with his mechanical projects. Since Anne is the eldest of three girls and Margie an only child, they are both tickled to have a brother and don't quite know how to manage him. Os felt that it was rather a burden to have three sisters but he finds it has its advantages, too – he isn't the boy not to make the most of them either! Wetherill has thoroughly enjoyed the companionship of sisters, too, so that we are quite content that this particular job fell to us.

Letter: October 15, 1951

Our little conglomeration is getting along quite well – there was a bit of a flurry when Margie thought Os was paying too much attention to another girl. When I told her she had to earn any priority, she recognized the reasonableness of that – and the fact that she had an inside track by living together.

I was mighty pleased with them all, the day Park Johnson[34] came to lunch. I had explained to them that Park wears a hearing aid and if they made their usual amount of noise during the meal it would be very trying for him. They were so quiet that, at first, Park didn't even realize that they were at their separate table.

Letter: November 18, 1951

So often Wetherill and Os please me by their nice friendliness to guests, but Margie and Anne can be such backward little sticks. They have not been accustomed to much supervision while up here at

34. R. Park Johnson was a Presbyterian missionary visiting from Lebanon. Two years later, our first night after leaving Tehran was spent with Park and his family in Beirut.

school so that it hasn't been easy for them. They have always lived in adult households and gone their own little ways. Both are now getting better marks than before and numerous missionaries have mentioned how much better behaved they are. The poor tykes need someone to look out for them – goodness knows I do too little. That is one of the sorrows of our situation: I don't have enough time for the children, but it is fun to have more of a household.

Letter: December 2, 1951

Had a bad accident last Sunday. Anne in her flighty way snapped a sweater at Wetherill, a button hit one of Wetherill's front teeth and broke about a ¼ of it off. I was simply sick about it. The dentist evened it off, said it might grow some and when her teeth were straightened some could be taken off the other front tooth to make them look more alike. It was awfully hard for me to be nice to Anne, especially since she took it very lightly. For several days I pointed out some of the heedless things she did that might also cause tragedy and I think at last she is aware of the seriousness of what she has done and that it was avoidable.

Letter: December 4, 1951

We found that Anne had a completely broken-down tooth which had abscessed. We don't get paid for things like holding a child's hand during an ordeal of that kind – there isn't any kind of pay for that. Since Anne didn't know that the tooth was out even when the extraction and scraping was all done, I am sure that her screaming was nerves not pain but when it was over I had to sit down in a hurry. Dr. Arfea was wonderfully quiet and patient, keeping all instruments out of her line of vision. A little present afterward and Anne was anxious to go back for another visit!!!

Letter: January 6, 1952

Anne and Margie are back with us and Mrs. Payne has Jean, Anne's sister, who has entered first grade. Having promised to take her, Mrs. P. tried to foist the child onto me, but I wouldn't foist since Jean is in school only in the morning.

[It must have been hard on the children of missionaries who lived in the hinterland because of their uncertain and frequently changing living arrangements during the school year. However, I don't remember hearing them complain about it. Wetherill and I were delighted to have Margie and Anne's company.]

Letter: January 29, 1952

Margie got thru measles with very little trouble and we hope Anne is going to escape – this is the 14th day and still no signs of trouble. There was one night that was a humdinger. At the height of Margie's discomfort Anne's tummy became upset. She worked awfully hard to make it a good thing for she had not been getting much attention. Osborne and I took turns getting up until about the 12th time I realized there was something unnatural about Anne's distress. Hardheartedly I told her that was enough, I didn't want any more of it – and there was no more! But Margie was awake by then and it took a while to get her quiet. The next day Anne was just as lively as ever and Margie's fever began to drop but Osborne and I were a little wilted.

Letter: January 11, 1953

Margie and Os had a party "buffet supper and dance" the invitation read!! It was awfully nice that the hostess told Osborne she was much impressed with how mannerly Os is! Os decided maybe he was growing up some, too – bless him. He reported that he danced with <u>all</u> the girls and one told him she thought he was nice. She is probably spoofing him but it did him good.

Letter: January 25, 1953

We had a nerve-racking time on Friday when all three girls played in Eleanor's piano recital. I hadn't been able to get Margie and Wetherill to knuckle down to hard practice. Wetherill just didn't have time – she has so much homework – and Margie had chosen something that she wasn't quite capable of playing. Her timing is much better than it used to be but she has a bad habit of repeating when she makes a mistake. She didn't realize what I was talking about until I counted as she played her four-line piece and found that she replayed thirteen times. Then she got down to work and stumbled thru without more than five repetitions.

Wetherill was very nervous though she didn't show it. Her pieces were both quite fast with difficult runs and she got thru them but flubbed the last note in her second piece which made her furious. She is anxious for another try and I think I won't have so much trouble getting her to practice. She now realizes what I meant by being better than perfect – under stress you break down if you have just reached perfection.

Letter: February 21, 1953

I feel completely taken down today because I've caught Anne out in a bold lie. It makes me sick and yet so thankful that my own children are the soul of honesty. Os pleased me so on Friday – I forgot to send word outside before we started our Quaker Meeting. He came in late and when the girls left (the children stay only half the time) Os stayed on until the end. It showed on honesty and self-discipline that was very nice. If I could only instill in Anne that sort of thing!

Oh it will be such a relief not to have other people's children to train. If I could just treat them as boarders it would be less wearing but when they are here more than they are home I feel an obligation.

Letter: April 13, 1953

Louise McNair is just the age little Eleanor Cresson will be when we first see her. Wetherill is getting to be something of a babysitter and wondered the other day how one mother is enough for a baby – it had taken both Wetherill and Margie to deal with one of Louise's emergencies!

Letter from Mary Wild: May 3, 1953

[As we were preparing to leave Iran, Anne's mother, Mary, wrote:] I believe you are due to be leaving for the States sometime this month, and I am writing to wish you all God's very best wherever you may be going next – and also to thank you for looking after Anne all the time you have been here. I know it has not been an easy job, and I am most grateful to you for accepting the responsibility – and incidentally for making it possible for me to stay out on the mission field at a time when it would have been not at all good for me to have been separated from my husband. I wonder what you are hoping to do next? Do you intend to return to Iran after your furlough, or do you have somewhere else in mind?

Chapter 6: Wetherill and Os

Letter: August 9, 1951

Sunday Wetherill conducted the Sunday School opening service with more composure than I could have mustered. Os told the story of Moses. A number of people have mentioned what an unusual vocabulary he has. He seems to have his great Granddad Edward's feeling for words.

But what a rascal! Last night Os finished his main course and was ready to leave the table to read until we caught up. When I told him to wait for dessert Eleanor [Engeman] added "Relax boy, relax." Osborne was called to the phone and a little later discovered that Os had slid down under the table and was stretched out carefully between our feet. "You told me to relax," he chortled to Eleanor and how he laughed when she blushed with surprise and confusion for none of us had noticed his disappearance, except Wetherill.

This week Osborne and Os went for a day long trip to a coal mine up a beautiful valley and climbing three hills. They were coal dusty and tired when they got back. We had tea for six or seven people that day. Wetherill didn't go because she will have a week's trip with the Buchers and their young people's group.

Letter: July 31, 1951

Wetherill asked to write the birthday letters on the 27th, since we missed getting them out before. Typically, she poked so that only Tiddo's[35] was finished but it is quite a nice little letter, don't you think? We talked about the birthday people – in fact, we had ice cream. It is usually a birthday treat and there have been so many here this month that we have reveled in ice cream. Ruth Elder makes perfect stuff.

Letter: August 23, 1951

John and Ruth Elder have been called home and they have

35. Tiddo, also called Aunt Melligo, was Rebecca's sister, Melda Mary Shannon, a librarian in the Port Authority of New York City. Wetherill and I carefully memorized her address: 57 Horatio Street, NYC. If we were ever permanently separated from our parents, that is where we would go or send word.

closed their house leaving many of their books with us and THE PIANO. It was home when Wetherill returned from her trip and she didn't know whether to spend time in her new room with its rosebud curtains or at the piano.

Letter: September 9, 1951

It was ever so nice to have such a pleasant meeting [with the Carletons who came on holiday with their daughter and two teachers from a school in Aleppo, Syria.] I think one reason Mrs. Carleton was so ready to accept us was because she thought the children were so well-behaved. "They've had training – it shows," she told me, and I was surprised to hear it because, though we are often proud of our two, we are almost as often desperate. Os has the bit in his teeth a good part of the time and even Wetherill is no pushover, sweet-tempered as she is.

But when Os has a project on hand, what energy! He had to move himself into Eleanor's vacated room with no help from me due to the teachers' meeting and the Wilds arriving on the same day. He moved the furniture to suit himself, tacked up airplanes he had made, put in his Scouting equipment, arranged his desk and has "a real boy's room", as he claims. It is neat and well-arranged and <u>finished</u>! The lad has his good points!

Wetherill loves her music. Practiced scales for over an hour and a half yesterday, for the sheer love of it!! Rick claims she will be able to play hymns in no time.

Letter: October 21, 1951

Whew, the time until Os' birthday is getting shorter and shorter. He thought it would be nice to have a group go to the usual Thursday soccer game and then come to supper but Saturday morning I heard that there was to be a game on Tuesday and not on Thursday. "How too bad," I told the goalie, "Os was expecting to celebrate his birthday with a game." When I went to school that evening to chaperone a dance the captain of the soccer team came over and told me that they had arranged a special game so that Os wouldn't be disappointed!!! Of course the boys love to play but it just shows what a nice, thoughtful bunch we have.

Letter: November 12, 1951

This morning Wetherill came down and giggled that she thought I might not be too pleased, but she was borrowing one of my blouses! It was a pink one whose sleeves had shrunk to be rather short for me though I still wore it. Imagine my surprise to find that the shoulders fit Wetherill perfectly and it is only in the length of arm that I surpass her!! Osborne warns me that I'll be having my clothes borrowed from now on and must resign myself to the fact.

Letter: Christmas Card, 1951

It has been a relief to have only our family in the house. Wetherill said, last night, that it was such fun to play with Os alone. They have good times! Isn't it wonderful that they are so fond of each other?

One day when we were having a Farsi lesson in our dining room. Wetherill had given a report on Afghanistan and wore her costume. She came home carrying a pewter samovar in one arm and a brass pitcher and bowl in the other. Her black *chador* with its ornament hanging in the middle of her forehead, earrings dangling and tinkling on either side of her lovely face made a strikingly beautiful picture. Our Farsi teacher, who has a lovely daughter himself, gasped and kissed Wetherill on the forehead. I wish I might have a painting of Wetherill as she looked then.

Os came in later and such a contrast! Nothing ethereal about him! But so sturdy and straightforward, with a gleam of mischief and cordiality in his flashing dark eyes. He has such a sense of the comic. When he was introduced to a 6' 3½" man he stepped up and shook hands, rearing back his head and lifting his eyebrows. He didn't spoil the effect by saying a word. It was perfect pantomime.

Letter: January 29, 1952

We discovered that Os is nearsighted and he now goes around with a pair of round tortoise rimmed glasses which make him look quite amusing. He loves them! I do hope that this will be a temporary, growth adjustment and not a permanent affliction.

Letter: March 16, 1952

Wetherill's passport picture is one of the loveliest she has ever had taken. When she saw it she said, "Why, how pretty!" I told her that she was pretty and she replied, "I didn't know that I looked like that!" It shows how grown up Wetherill looks now – she is four feet ten and a half inches tall!

I am so glad that she is growing up without being conscious of how often people notice her looks. The other day Joe and Bernice Cochran had lunch with us. Joe said something to Wetherill in his gently teasing way. Wetherill quipped right back and looked at Joe with a face so dazzlingly full of sparkle that it threw Joe completely off base and he had to let her have the best of that sortie! But most of the time she is still a frolicsome little girl who is ready to pinch hit if the boys don't have enough players and hasn't yet outgrown hide and seek.

Not to leave Os out of the picture – he is beginning to grow, too. Today when he was taking up the collection in church Tiger Kennedy, a Fulbright man,[36] leaned over to me and said, "Os always looks so businesslike when he does that." He is quite sober about it and gives people a friendly but very dignified smile when he meets their glances. This afternoon he was posting our personal accounts under Osborne's direction! But he shouts, clomps on the stairs and hates to wash his hands so he is normal, too.

Tonight when Os was looking over my passport application he noticed Father's name and in his usual quick way he decided that he would have a son named Thomas Berry Cresson! He wants an Osborne III also. Hope he has them.

Letter: March 2, 1952

The Second Secretary's wife at our Embassy has been teaching this year and is now taking Mrs. Young's place. She is aware of a good bit and told me the other day to see that Os has free swing with his imagination, that she felt he had such a creative mind and such a wonderful feeling for words. That his verbal and written expressions

36. The Fulbright Program provided grants for international educational exchange. (https://us.fulbrightonline.org)

were exceptional. She is a PhD in psychology. It doesn't mean that he isn't an imp! His clowning drives Osborne wild.

Letter: May 19, 1952

Osborne thought you would be interested in a conversation I had with the children recently. They sat on the end of my bed and began to talk of the teacher who was so cruel to Os. That lad had done some figuring and astounded me with his findings. He decided that she must have something in her background to explain her personality peculiarities – and that it might be her physique which is large, that boys didn't date her when she was in school, that some teacher had mistreated her, or that there was some family conflict. Now if that isn't a pretty clear bit of ten-year-old thinking! Personally I think he may be right on all scores. He thought it might be good if some "sweet" kind of person like Henrietta Gurney talked to her and tried to help her iron out her problems and understand herself!! Sometimes I could abandon all hope of Os because of his stubborn willfulness and then I get a glimpse of such straight thinking and goodwill that I take hope.

Letter: April 4, 1952

Wetherill went on a two-day hike with the Girl Scouts – they "hiked" in trucks to a garden a few miles out of town! They slept out, did their own cooking, scrambled around some foothills and came back with sunburned noses for the leaves were not out enough to cast a shade, though there were trees in the garden.

Os turned down the suggestion of having some boys come to visit him while the girls were all away and seemed to thoroughly enjoy himself practicing tennis shots against the compound wall and playing with the collection of boys who came each day to play at Community School. He is an avid reader. I have more sympathy with him than has Osborne, for I remember how hard it was to leave a book. I have trouble that way still when bedtime comes.

Letter: May 19, 1952

Os is pretty pet minded and since he is so swamped with girls in this compound we have let him indulge a bit. So far there are Demavand (named for Iran's highest mountain) who is called Demi or Demijon which means darling Demi. He is a fuzzy pup who hasn't yet decided to be black or white and is still gray with black spots. He has a cute wire-haired terrier face and is an awful scaredy. He is still at the chewing stage and the children have banished him from the house until he outgrows it.

Next we acquired two ducks for the irrigating pond. Os bought them with his own money and named the black-and-white female Shab (Night) and the tan speckled male Sobh (Morning). All the children are hoping for ducklings!!!

Yesterday we broke down and let Os acquire another dog. There is a woman in town who has become a shelter for mistreated and stray dogs. Mrs. Yavru took Os to see her and Rex has joined the household. He is ten months old, about the size of our Española Caversham but of a handsome auburn shade that somewhat indicates his Irish setter mother and his yellow dog mongrel father. He seems to be a quiet, affectionate dog and didn't disturb us until Os woke up to take him out this morning. Quiet in that he doesn't bark but he has lots of pep and loves to romp with the children and Demi. We are careful to avoid translating his name into Farsi because there is still a strong Muslim feeling about the lowliness of a dog. One does not name a canine for a friend in Iran. Having a dog named King might be grossly misunderstood if it were made obvious.

I rather wonder what is coming next in our menagerie!

Letter: July 10, 1952

Mr. Ware, the British Bank Manager, told me that at the garden party where he was stationed to receive people, he had greeted 176 and was standing around rather alone when Os sauntered up and inquired, "Don't you find life boring sometimes?" He was frightfully amused at the originality and aplomb of our 10-year-old. And everyone thinks Wetherill is such a lovely little lady. She has a sweet manner.

Letter: September 3, 1952

Maybe we didn't tell you of some excitement with Wetherill's first formal the other day. I've never sewed so hard in all my life and

Batool helped sew on the bows at the last minute. She and Yeksabet, Osborne and Os and I all supervised Wetherill's finishing touches and we all agreed that the result was just about perfection.

Osborne and Os escorted Wetherill to her party. The latter went along simply because he was so proud of his sister! Starting out with such pleasure in her dress Osborne feared the party might be a letdown but she had a lovely time and didn't seem at all disconcerted when one of her dance partners tried a new step and she didn't follow perfectly. "I guess I didn't do too badly, for just learning. Felix didn't mind and it was fun," Wetherill remarked about it!

Letter: September 22, 1952

We came back from the Caspian a day earlier than expected since it began to rain and Os to wheeze, though by the night we arrived in town he had no difficulty. Then a hard day of play was too much for him and in the middle of the night he began again so we kept him quiet for two days.

Os got up in time for dinner since Zorick[37] was coming to try him out on the violin. What a thrill it was for me, too! He tested quite well on his ear and though his bow wobbled all over he recognized the off tones and was so pleased and anxious to do more he almost took the violin to bed with him. Then he decided to leave it downstairs "so I'll have to dress before I begin to play." Since we have three piano students and one violin (not counting me) we are going to have a more or less musical household.

Letter: December 2, 1952

Wetherill's latest "boy friends" are the two brothers we met at the Caspian. She likes the younger, brighter one best but the 15-year-old is taller. It is their party she is going to Saturday. Her dancing isn't smooth yet but is improving and I shall be glad that she has had experience when we return to U.S. – You don't mind my raving do you?

37. Zorick Dilanian was a violinist, teacher and friend. I heard him playing the violin in a concert and instantly knew I wanted to make sounds like that. It was an important part of my life through high school. After that I seemed to have reached my limits and I didn't continue with the violin.

I try to be modest to others but Wetherill is lovely – an Iranian asked us "Is that fairy child yours?"

Of course I can't rave about one child without showing that the other has just as much that is interesting and endearing. I just received a letter from a literary agent to whom I sent an article. She liked it and suggests a book on Afghanistan! When I told Os he was all interest and sympathy so I explained that I would like to do fiction, too, since there is a limit to the travel market. With his usual quirk of humor he said "Fine – I do a lot of day dreaming. I'll give you ideas. I'll stay home from school to day dream. Boy, what a job – $10 a day for dreaming!!" he has a wonderful turn of phrase and an astounding vocabulary.

Letter: January 11, 1953

Wetherill is twelve and a half today and all grown up. When I was digging out a Kotex for her last night she remarked "I don't think I'm the least bit pleased about all this!" She was off to an 8th grader's party where the boyfriend she shared with Margy Gurney turned up enthusiastic about another girl! Of course that sort of thing is unpleasant but Wetherill isn't the girl to go into a tailspin over it.

Letter: March 7, 1953

I was quite surprised when Os told me one day when there had been so few in school that they did no lessons, that he had decided life was very much more interesting and happy when you had a lot to do and did it!! Now I understand why teachers need more holidays than people who work in offices – there is much more strain in keeping one jump ahead of a class. You have to be ready to veer with the tempo of the students, and you don't feel that tempo without effort on your part.

Letter: April 13, 1953

Last night we had quite a family musical – Osborne was the conductor, Wetherill and Os played a duet and I held the music!! It astounds me that Os continues to have so much enthusiasm for the violin. He loves it and puts in good hard work on it. I have much more respect for all violinists now that I have seen what it takes. Wetherill's music is now at the point where she is playing simplified versions of famous melodies and it gives me a lift to hear her play things that I remember hearing Ret[38] play when I was very young.

I just thought how tickled Granddad would have been at his great-grandchildren's interest in music.

Letter: May 11, 1953

Ret, you are going to have the best time with the children! They really are awfully sweet and interesting, and developing quite nicely. Os told me the other day that Wetherill was "sticking paper, to the boys" because she was so sweet and he didn't blame the boys one bit! I thought that was quite a compliment from a brother.

Letter draft: c. 1954

Wetherill has declared that if she can't get back to Iran any other way she will have it written into her marriage contract that her husband shall take her there! She is enough of an Iranian to forget that Americans don't have marriage contracts.

38. Ret was Rebecca's mother, Rebecca Edwards Shannon, who lived in Morristown, NJ. Her love of music came from her Welsh grandparents. Once, when I was in high school, Grandma Rettie sat down at our piano and played the melodies she had heard at a Philadelphia Orchestra concert a few hours earlier!

Chapter 7: Rebecca and Osborne

Letter: September 16, 1951

Dick Irvine [the school principal], who has a calm and quiet voice and is excellent in dealing with people, has said over and over that he was duly thankful to have Osborne who is so good at organization and watching details. They work together well and have a very united approach to our problems.

Letter: November 12, 1951

Had just time to eat supper and dash off to another lecture and then I came home and read until late. Stupid of me, but with such an occupied life I find that I crave the outlet of reading more than ever, and there is the excuse that I should read some of the books I don't know in order to interest students in them, and decide whether they are appropriate for our shelves.

Letter: January 6, 1952

Our fifteenth wedding anniversary [on January 1st, 1952] was a bit of a frost as far as I was concerned. Was running a fever and felt wretched so did not go to the Mission Open House which was held in the school auditorium. Many Iranian friends were there. Both of our servants helped with serving tea and Wetherill took my place quite capably.

Later in the week we went to a huge party with the Irvines at the Indonesian Embassy where five of the Community School boys made up a very creditable dance band. Osborne and I had great fun dancing and one of the guests spoke to us when he noticed the Afghan sheepskin vest I was wearing – he is at the Afghan Embassy and knows numerous people whom we know. There have been other parties, including tea at Yeksabet's house and a concert with Chuck Swan and the Kennedys (Beirut University, on leave as a Fulbright scholar).

Letter: March 16, 1952

The children planned my birthday all by themselves – with violets strewn all around my place at the table, small bouquets and handmade gifts since they couldn't get out to shop. They decided that I would prefer a "family" party rather than a large tea which they thought of first – I was so glad that they decided that way! It has been a little wearing to be nurse, hostess, mother, librarian and head of the house but I am a tough character and have been feeling stronger right along and now feel quite normal. Last night for the first time Osborne was able to manage his middle of the night medicine by himself so I had a better night's rest.

Letter: May 19, 1952

Though having troubles with moving and mumps on the one hand, there happens on the other hand something like little Grace Payne's faithfulness during the long weeks of my illness. She has come in almost every day with books for me to read, starting with her own novel on Iran, *The Unveiling*. It is a book of excellent local color done with utmost sympathy and to me a surprising amount of story-feeling. Poor thing told me one day when I told her of my appreciation for her care, that she had always thought that she could love me very dearly if I would let her. Made me feel quite contrite for all the times that I have been impatient with her peculiar ways. There is good and bad in all of us, if we could just concentrate more on nice parts and ignore the irritations, but then you begin to wonder if you are being used for a goat and if that is weakening to your character. Awful muddle.

Since I have been getting through almost a book a day, except during the worst of the mumps, I've managed to read quite a bit and thoroughly enjoy that part of it. I am missing quite a bit of school.

Letter: June 24, 1952

Osborne and I were invited with the Gurneys (former missionaries now with USIE) to chaperone the eighth-grade final party. They had planned it quite well and we did enjoy it though we had to smile at how much more juvenile they were than the high school students! Osborne had to rescue the master of ceremonies who announced a contest to see who was the best dancing couple. Ara mentioned a prize and then realized that they had none to offer. Osborne had them get one of the huge bun-shaped chicken sandwiches that were part of the refreshments and presented it with a flourish, getting the rewarded couple to stand up and bite on it from opposite ends much to the amusement of the other youngsters.

Letter: January 3, 1953

We had intended to get letters off to various Friends Schools, looking for jobs next year but Osborne had to close the accounts – another silly mission treasurer ruling – and we didn't get it done. I wish that Osborne could find something like he is doing here for he really is good at business management. He usually balances his books right on the nose at the first crack – this time was more trouble because he had started to teach Jane Thomson how to do it and that caused some errors. Osborne is now Treasurer of Community School with full financial responsibility which is going to be an awful headache because Dick goes ahead and makes commitments without consultation.

(Writing this has been hard going because our little friend the dwarf, Navart, is doing the unmarrieds' ironing in the study and she is such an amusing talker I can't get much done!)

Letter: February 17, 1953

While the Tabriz missionaries were here the Gurneys invited them and Osborne and me to meet Dr. and Mrs. Cree from Iowa who just arrived to go to the Tabriz area and work on Point Four[39] agricultural education. Osborne thought perhaps we were the comic relief! When we discovered that the Crees had read one of the Zoradnicks' letters we arranged to go to Shemiran with them so that they might have a chance to visit. As we suspected Dr. Cree was much interested and pleased with John Z's attitude and knowledge.

In the conversation I suggested that Osborne might do some speaking for Near East Foundation when we returned to USA and so we arranged without further delay to spend next Friday at the villages to see the projects and gather material. We feel that the work being done by this organization is really vital – they had a louse of a director until recently and now things are so much better the Zoradnicks' are

39. Point Four was a U.S. State Department program for technical assistance in developing countries. It later became the Agency for International Development (AID).

planning to return here after a month's holiday in USA next fall.

Diary: March 10-11, 1953

My 43rd birthday was as nice as the preceding three had been heartbreaking.[40] Navart and I had arranged to shop for material she will use for table mats she is to embroider for me. Osborne and Os went along to find a birthday gift for me. En route we stopped at Daveed's at USIE and found some Zanjan beads made into earrings which Osborne got as Wetherill's gift for me- she was in bed with a cold. Also found some small brass items for gifts to take back to the U.S. The two Os's went off while Navart and I got material for a silk skirt for Wetherill (maroon watered silk very pretty) and white for table mats. Then we found some very nice fruit knives and forks with Isfahan design and a grooved edge which will go very well with our Lady Diane silver. Plan to use them for butter spreaders and cocktail forks as needed.

Next morning I went into Wetherill's room where everyone gathered but I didn't realize that Os had taken his violin from behind the curtain until he began to play "Happy Birthday." He did it extremely well. Bless his heart he had been practicing for months, whenever I was out of the house!

Letter: April 20, 1953

We had a terror of a basketball game. The coach of the opposing team insisted upon being one of the referees and he never saw a foul against his own team even when our boys stopped play after obvious fouls – arms wrapped around them and such. Our team did a marvelous job of keeping their tempers and my pet, Cyrus Baktiar, the captain, was a wonderful influence. The score was nip and tuck all the way and my library assistant threw a basket in the last seven seconds to win the game. Osborne was so excited he jumped up and down and flapped his arms, then threw them around me and kissed me which was a dubious example to set right in front of the grandstands!

40. The heartbreak the year before was probably the death of little Mark Irvine as well as problems following Ezmari's visit to Tehran and sickness in our family. Rebecca's two birthdays before that, in Kabul, came during conflict between Osborne and the Ministry of Education concerning his employment.

Letter: May 19, 1953

I must say that I didn't relish the prospect when Osborne mentioned the possibility of his hurrying on to the U.S. ahead of us. I have been spoiled having him take care of border crossings, passports and money. Os would manfully do his level best but it is convenient to have Osborne!

Letter: May 19, 1953

I don't believe that Osborne would object to speaking [in the U.S. for the Near East Foundation] even without the $50-100 bait. Me – I'm different – it has been so long since I have done any of it that it would be awfully hard on me. As long as I didn't have to stand up – if I could just chat I could spiel off but my knees shake when I have to stand up and look down on people.

Letter: May 10, 1953

It wasn't until we went to church this morning that any of us realized that it was Mother's Day. We thought of you, Ret, and I decided to write to you on the day even though you might not get it for a week. As Dickin[41] mentioned in his sermon – a day that was started as a purely business venture has a real and good purpose. It is fine to stop and think on one day, concentrated, about how much your mother means to you. It is nice to have one you are proud of and enjoy.

The church service was one of the most inspiring I have ever attended. There wasn't any sentimental patter – but Dickin's mother must be a mighty fine person because Dickin has such a high concept of the responsibilities and opportunities of motherhood.

Before the end of the service Wetherill and Os had reached over and we were all four holding hands in an intense realization of what it meant to be a family. Dickin has a fairly deep, quiet voice, tells a story very effectively with a nice sense of humor and kept the whole congregation entirely alert.

41. Leon A. Dickinson, Jr. was the new pastor in the Presbyterian Mission in Tehran. He became Rebecca's lifelong friend.

Home Life

Overleaf: *In front of our home in Tehran, Wetherill carrying Margie, Os walking up, and Rebecca just visible in the pathway.*

Wetherill, beside a tree, in front of our first home in the Central Compound of the Presbyterian Mission in Tehran.

Wetherill, with Demivand behind her, on the porch of our second home, in the New Compound that included Community School and some staff housing.

Os with Shaheen and her mother, Ruhie, who did our laundry.

Os, Shaheen and Ruhie on the steps of our second home.

Navart and Rebecca used to go shopping and work on projects together. She was such enjoyable company that Rebecca sometimes forgot what they were working on!

Daisy, a Community School student from Iraq, models traditional village clothing.

Os and Mashtali, the gardener in the Central Compound. We are both in our Sunday clothes. When the trees were planted the compound was on the outskirts of the city, but it is now near the center.

Gulam Hossain, the gardener in the New Compound, was an artist in his work. He worked hard and rarely smiled.

Rebecca, Wetherill and her friend, Margy Gurney, and Osborne in front of the church in Central Compound.

A gathering of school teachers and staff on the porch of our second house. The four Cressons were in matching shirts and skirts made by Rebecca for the trip to the U.S. from Iran. (They did help keep us together!)

We were watching Community School celebrations at the end of the school year.

The high life in Tehran, probably at an Embassy. Rebecca liked to wear local jewelry and items of clothing.

Wetherill and Os visiting the home of some of their schoolmates.

Wetherill and Os at the wedding of Tom and Eleanor McNair, their well-loved friends.

A formal dinner in an Iranian home.

Osborne and Rebecca square dancing in Tehran, with Os watching. Rebecca and Osborne found, or created, square dance groups wherever they lived.

Ezmari, our friend from Afghanistan who visited us in Tehran. In a few days he was converted from Islam to Christianity which was prohibited for Afghans. Rebecca was extremely unhappy about this.

Two of Rebecca and Osborne's favorite people: Leon Dickinson, a pastor, and Hykon Sahakian, a teacher.

Chapter 8: Two Homes

[Our first home was a large house in the Central Compound. After a year we moved into another large house, this one in the New Compound across town.]

Letter: July 31, 1951

Yesterday Osborne and the children spent the whole day with a borrowed truck getting our possessions back from the other compound.[42] The Irwins will move tomorrow and then we will be in our own house, at last. The Irwins are leaving some furniture, curtains and rugs which will be a tremendous help. We will take over their servants. Batool, who has worked for missionaries for years, sounds like an acknowledged gem. She became a Christian several years ago. Mohammad is a cheerful young cook without the stability of Batool but a pleasant boy who is willing, likes children and may develop into a good servant. We released the other pair we had expected to have – quite a bit of politicking by interested missionaries on both sides, with us in the middle, but I think we made the best decision without hurting too many feelings. The next month isn't going to be easy – a household to settle, servants' vacation due, canning, sewing, curtains and reupholstering, lesson plans to formulate and as much Farsi as we can cram in before September.

Holiday Letter: December 7, 1951

We were given a large house so that we might harbor the two boarding students who came to school from the provincial mission stations. Our two new daughters are Margaret Frame whose mother and step-father are doctors at the Rasht Mission Hospital, and Anne Wild whose father is a doctor in the British Mission Hospital at Isfahan where her mother also works.[43]

Our house is a two-story yellow brick with a fair-sized living room, study, small den for the children's books and games, dining

42. Our truck had been unloaded in the New Compound, but we, and the school, did not move there until a year later.

43. These were Rolla and Adelaide Hoffman, and Peter and Mary Wild.

room, pantry and kitchen. Upstairs we have four bedrooms, two dressing rooms and a bathroom with a long mummy case of a tin tub. It is a fairly efficient arrangement. The wide end butts into the hot water tank where a kerosene heater provides a slow supply of heat. The small end hangs over an open trough with an outlet so that all you have to do to empty the tub is pull the plug and tip the tub to get the last drops of water out. The toilets (one down and one upstairs) are just outside the main part of the house and have regulation seats but no flush arrangement. You have to throw the water in by hand.

I was aghast at the system when I first saw it on our visit two years ago but found that when there was talk of spending a large amount on improved plumbing a number of us thought plumbing was not so awfully important after all, in comparison with the slum project in south Tehran.

Just this week our stoves have been installed – kerosene burning and such an improvement over the little tin wood-and-coal burning arrangements of Kabul (providing our kerosene supply holds out!) Our furniture is mostly inherited from the former school principal and one of our greatest joys is the piano which John and Ruth Elder have lent us.

We Went to School in Tehran

The kitchen was equipped with a kerosene stove which was a great improvement over the charcoal stove of Afghanistan but it proceeded to exhibit me as a complete ignoramus by smoking furiously in spite of all my efforts to turn it off. By the time we called in the houseboy from next door the kitchen was black and I was ready to cook on charcoal. The houseboy taught me to keep wet rags wrapped around the burners to cool them in summer weather but after we acquired mission servants of long standing, Yeksabet and Batool, I kept my distance from the kerosene stove.

We had experiences with our kerosene heating stoves, too, when cold weather came. The old living room stove was removed and we put in a different one. That afternoon we were entertaining for tea and I expected to use a small hand stove for heat. Batool decided when she brought in the tea that the room was not warm enough. While I poured tea she filled the tank of the big stove with odorous kerosene. The odor lingered and we soon discovered that kerosene was pouring onto the floor. We stuck a flower vase under the leak and sent for the handyman. Because there was no other warm room in the house, our tea was, thereafter, a riot of smells and sounds as we huddled at one end of the room and shouted above the hammering on metal, clank of pipe, and complaint of the stove as it was ignominiously dismantled and carried out.

We looked a little sooty and disheveled and Batool would not leave us like that. She mopped up the soot, adding to the confusion of tea-drinking, and had Ismael bring back the repaired stove which was triumphantly lit as our guests made their weary farewells!

[After a year in the central mission compound, we moved 1½ miles across Tehran to the new compound where the school would be.]

Letter: June 24, 1952

I am writing from the study in our new home – yes, we are all moved. It happened very suddenly and much to the surprise of the Ports, I think. When I had been out of bed three days [after recovering from mumps], Wetherill came into our room at 6:30 in the morning to tell me that she had moved Anne from her bed into Wetherill's to get her away from Margie for Anne had mumps! I had expected to go to school that day but knew that I couldn't do that and take care of Anne, too, so I stayed home with doctor's instructions not to do more than a half day's work for a week.

That evening, after station meeting, I was told that the Ports had said they could move in three days or not until mid-July – both Osborne and I said "Fine, we'll move in three days", and by gory, we did!! Our servants were marvelous and carried most of the load, for I could pack for only a few minutes at a time and would then have to lie down. I felt pretty inadequate the day I sat on the floor trying to summon strength enough to push a feather quilt into a bureau drawer!

Funny things happened – I carefully packed all the First Aid equipment into a metal wastepaper basket and put it where I would know where to find it in case of an emergency. Batool found it and dumped the whole business out, thinking it was trash! She was able to retrieve some of it though the antiseptic bottles were all broken.

As it turned out we couldn't even get our second load out of the compound because a tree fell across the main gate and it took all afternoon to get it dislodged and cut up. All the men, including Os, had a lovely time trying to pull the tree off the gatepost and it was Osborne's suggestion that finally did the trick – engineering training comes in handy in odd ways sometimes.

Since all our furniture was on the porch ready for the second load and Osborne had to go to a school committee meeting, I decided to be the guard of our possessions – my jewelry and Osborne's camera were hidden in bureau drawers. As I started to crawl over some of the furniture to get to one of the beds which was complete with mattress, I discovered Batool looking for a rug to use for sleeping since all her possessions were packed, too. I asked if her son would like to sleep on the bed on the porch. She replied that Hassan would not be a good guard because he "slept like a stone," but that Mashtali, the gardener, had agreed to sleep there. I expressed my thanks and escaped to my bedroom where I laughed heartily to think what would have happened if I hadn't discovered the servant's plan and had been peacefully sleeping when Mashtali tried to climb into the same bed! Wouldn't we have been a surprised pair? To appreciate the joke you should see Mashtali who is no older than Osborne but is bent, wrinkled and awfully grumpy looking.

Batool and Ruhie (our laundress) went up to the new house early the second morning. Yeksabet was sick with food poisoning and I supervised moving out the last things, including Anne who went to spend two days with Grace Payne before going to Isfahan. Beth Muller fed us the last two days which was a very pleasant help. By the time I got up to the hospital compound my two servants were in a state over the conditions they had found. They would not let me settle a room until they had cleaned it three times!!!

The first night Wetherill came in most disgusted. She had walked from her room to the bathroom to get a drink of water and had to wash her feet before she could get back into bed! I had had my servants sweep the whole house that we were leaving and was I mad when Ella Mae told Osborne that she had never seen as dirty a house as the one we left! I shouldn't have been mad because I honestly know that our windows were clean and that she could have walked barefoot all over the house, but you don't like having lies told about you – especially when you were keeping a secret of the liar's own failings.

It rather soured me on this new house but now I am getting over it and discover that it is really a pleasant place to be. The rooms are large and open with floor-length windows in every room so that you lie in bed and look out into the tree tops – a lovely feeling.

We have two rugs – both Tabriz made. One is the type usually exported with a wide border and center medallion. The colors are unusual, for Persian rugs, being rich jewel colors in green, rusty red and gold with a cream background instead of the more common blues and reds. The other rug is a typical product for domestic Iranian consumption. Its many kinds of deer, antelope and ibex combine with flowers, birds and fish against a dusty rose field to make a very interesting rug which is surprisingly attractive.

Our Afghan brass hubble bubble pipes make nice lamps, the Cresson clock and two brass plates Mrs. Yavru gave us as a house gift and our few but interesting pictures give the living room quite a genteel air even without curtains. The wide hall we have fixed with a couch and chair, tables and bookshelf into a dropping down spot which gives the entrance a welcoming look. We have also acquired a brass Iranian type samovar for tea parties. It has a rounder water container than the usual Russian samovar but we wanted to have something typical of this country. We also found some badly needed brass finger-bowls and a fairly good-sized tray to use for a coffee table, though we don't have legs for it yet.

Our Persian print curtains are the only ones we have that are long enough so curtain making is going to be a problem. I haven't gotten to it because rugs came first and then I went to bed for a week with what two of the holidaying mission doctors decided was malaria! Evidently getting too tired brought on a recurrence. Was I peeved? When I had so much to do. [Rebecca called this as her month of mumps, moving and malaria.]

Chapter 9: Food

Letter: August 23, 1951

People say that food prices are high in Tehran but our eggs are not 91¢ a dozen – they are 1 Toman[44], 2 Rials and 10 Shahi, or 25¢, for twenty!! Of course our eggs are neither candled, refrigerated nor cleaned and they are not packed in safety containers. We do pay 22¢ for English gelatin similar to Jell-O and a mark-up like that for anything that is not local. There is a big old bazaar where you can buy in wholesale lots, a bushel of vegetables at a time, but on our street there are several small shops that have vegetable stands at the edge of the sidewalk with bread, flour and such things.

The butcher shops are usually about 12 feet x 12 ft, open most of the way across the front, tiled around the other three walls, with a cutting counter and small ice refrigs. They look clean and neat and the food they sell is a shade more tender than the leather we chewed in Kabul. At one store we can get bacon, ham and pork products which are rather expensive but such a treat to us [but not eaten by strict Muslims.]

The national dishes are chalau and pilau – a little different from the variety we had in Kabul but very tasty.[45] In Afghanistan foreigners didn't eat *mawst* but everyone eats it here and Wetherill is delighted for she is very fond of it. It is like sour junket and goes well with rice dishes.

We also eat raw vegetables that have been carefully peeled or scrubbed [which we did not do in Afghanistan]. It is wonderful to crunch raw carrots again and I don't miss lettuce quite so much, having something raw to eat. It is possible to get store made cookies and the candy stores are just exactly like some of the flossy confectionery stores in the USA.

We Went to School in Tehran

The milkman came to our house on a bicycle with tin cans balanced on either side of the rear wheel. He dipped out our required

44. In the currency of Iran, one Toman was equal to 10 Rials, and one Rial equal to 20 Shahi. In 1952, one Toman was worth about 20¢ (U.S.).

45. Chalau is rice with a sauce poured over it, while pilau has the rice and other ingredients mixed and cooked together.

amount into the pan we provided. If Yeksabet and Batool were not in the kitchen he came in and found a pan for himself. His service even included lighting the stove and putting the milk on to boil, or setting it into the refrigerator if he thought the servants would not be back soon.

Lavash is also brought slung cross the rear wheel of a bike. It is paper-thin bread that we dried and crumbled as a substitute for wheat flakes, or toasted in place of crackers. The egg man carried his basket on his head and sometimes had such a high pyramid that it was a real feat of balance to avoid an eggy disaster.

"Do people really eat that many melons?" an American guest inquired when we passed a mound of melons almost head high and stretching twenty feet along the sidewalk. People do. The melons are sweetly delicious and not expensive. Nuts are plentiful, too, including walnuts, almonds and pistachios as well as nut-flavored squash and watermelon seeds.

Oranges are in the market only a short time and bananas very seldom but shiny red pomegranates are sold from early fall thru the winter. Fresh dates, though unpackaged and full of sticks, are more tasty than any American variety I have ever come across.

My favorite Iranian food is *fesenjan* chalau (pomegranate chicken or duck). It has tender fluffy rice with a topping of black, deadly looking stew made of pomegranate juice, walnuts and wild fowl. It is delectable but so murderous in appearance and strong in flavor that it takes a bold eater to appreciate it at the first try. [Yeksabet kept a piece of iron that she put in the pot with the sauce while it was cooking to produce the traditional black color.][46]

46. For a recipe for *fesenjan* chalau, and a lot of other fine dishes, see *In a Persian Kitchen* by Maideh Mazda (Rutland VT: Charles E. Tuttle, 1960).

Chapter 10: Health

Letter: November 12, 1951

All three girls have had colds – Margie catches them easily and passed them on when all three were sleeping in one room. Osborne was too tired to resist but Os and I have escaped so far. There are so many colds these days of changeable weather when you have to have heat part of the time and go from a warm to a cold room. Many families postpone heating as long as possible and the children bring colds to school.

Letter: March 2, 1952

Tragedy and illness have been very close to us. The day that Rolla Hoffman returned from his trip to New York with Judith Macomb, who is given only six months to live, Dick Irvine came running asking for Rolla. "Mark looks queer" he said. His little 17-month-old-boy has had asthma and pneumonia but had seemed to be improving. I went over to see if I could do anything.

That evening little Mark gave up the struggle.

The next morning Carol and I were delegated to care for flowers, Osborne, Bob Bucher, Chuck Swan and Rick Pond were pall bearers, Art conducted the service and Clem Scott saw that people got into the cars as Osborne had drawn up the list. Os did not go to the service, choosing instead to take care of little Jean Wild (Anne's sister). The service was very sweet and Art did a marvelous job. How he kept his voice so smooth throughout was exceptional. The little coffin was put in the station wagon, John Clinton drove, and five of us rode in there with Mr. Payne driving Dick and Mary Ann and the Mullers. Mark's little nursemaid stood beside me at the grave. I was much upset that we had to stand and watch the men fill the grave. Zahra broke down completely and I had to smother her sobs on my shoulder, that was the hardest thing of all.

Letter: March 2, 1952

Osborne went to bed with a fever as soon as we got home from the funeral. I went over that evening to the Irvines and then complications set in at home. The next day I spent at home taking care of Osborne and waiting for the doctor, a blood test etc. It looked as though Osborne was going to have malaria but it did not develop – a severe flu bug with chills and fever. The next morning Os had it and a few hours later Wetherill was in bed. I was coughing violently and when the Embassy nurse found I was running quite a fever she put me to bed in Wetherill's room so we had a men's ward and a women's ward. By Sunday Margie had a light touch! We are all well now but limping around like rags.

Beth and Mary Jo Cullen took good care of us. Yeksabet and Batool were so faithful, even to taking turns staying at night to bring us medicine in the wee small hours. Finally they found a Tabriz trained nurse for us and believe me we are glad to be passed this episode.

Letter: March 16, 1952

Our Men's Ward was revived. Three days after Osborne hobbled back to school he was back in bed with a half hour chill which shook the bed it was so hard. Burt Dyson, the Hamadan doctor, was in town on the way to Rasht. He administered Aralen and the fever dropped but pleurisy set in so that Osborne is still in bed and will stay there until next week when school will be closed for the New Year holiday and I can take him by air to Tabriz for rest and treatment at the hospital there. Arnold Schneider, the doctor up there, was a house guest of ours during the early days of this second bout and he wants to keep an eye on Osborne. He says that there is no sign of any further trouble but that if Osborne goes back to work too soon again he might be in for more serious complications. Arnold found that with such a severe pain in his side that he couldn't turn over, Osborne was still trying to work on the payroll. He said the only thing was to get Osborne out of town where he couldn't even be consulted.

Margie's parents, Rolla and Adelaide Hoffman, both doctors, were also house guests during this time so they consulted with Arnold and all three decided that the flu was really complicated with malaria though the blood test didn't show it. Today Osborne feels much better, the first time that I have felt really encouraged. Os also had a relapse with a week in bed but is hale and hearty now. There has been a regular epidemic in town with many relapses.

Letter: March 25, 1952

Since Joe Cochran is back in town this week, he checked Osborne and found him progressing well and recommended that we stay right here [rather than go to Tabriz]. It will be rather difficult to keep Osborne away from problems and from a guilty feeling that he is wasting time, now that his energy is returning, but I think that the doctors have thoroughly convinced him that rest is necessary until they say he may get back into circulation.

He is gaining weight – five pounds in ten days is not bad and brings him up to just about where he was, which is too little so we are shooting for more. He eats four eggs a day, malted milks and quite respectable meals and now that the sun is shining he is allowed to sit out on the upper porch in the spring warmth. There are flowering trees in the compound and a few early flowers so that there is a definite feeling of renewal at our house.

Letter: May 19, 1952

From the land of mumps – our greetings, birthday wishes for those to whom they are due, and sincere hopes that you avoid the kind of life we have been leading. Things could have been much worse, so we are duly thankful.

Wetherill got through her attack of mumps without much discomfort and quite on schedule. I took care of her with due precautions and would let no one else near her, but by the time she had been on her feet a few days I was in bed – my jaws didn't begin to swell for ten days but I was definitely out of commission. The swelling was not serious nor too uncomfortable but the hitch has been that one side refuses to subside. Our good friend Mary Jo, the Embassy nurse, says it is just that I was too rundown to throw off the infection and will have to keep quiet for as long as it takes the swelling to go down. Wetherill was an excellent little nurse, giving me baths, bringing up trays and even learning to change sheets with a patient in the bed! Osborne swelled up the day after I did but he had a very light touch and was on his feet within a few days, though the doctor kept him quiet for a week in order not to run into difficulties.

Less than a week later Clem Scott became ill, and so did Joy

Bucher. Since the Mullers were away – Clem lives in part of their house – there wasn't anyone to take care of him, except the little dwarf, Navart. I suggested that since Osborne was on his feet and Wetherill such a competent little nurse, Clem be moved over to our hospital, and much to everyone's surprise he put up no opposition. Clem moved into Os' room and stayed with us about ten days. He is such a fine fellow, so kindly, unassuming and pleasant in his very shy way that all were sorry when he moved back to his own quarters. It tickled me no end to hear Wetherill's technique when she popped in to take his trays or visit with him. The lass is developing quite a bit of poise and some facility at repartee – her role of hostess and nurse were both very adequately managed.

But there is one mighty fine report to make – Osborne can't button the top button of his pants!! He weighs 140 and is on the last notch of his belt! He is very much relieved that all the weight has not gone to his belt but is spread liberally all over his frame. His color is good and his pep is coming back, too. And he is going to need all the pep he has.

Chapter 11: Rebecca's Writing

[As a child Rebecca loved to read and write and she saw this as a way to help her family out of their financial difficulties. She studied writing in college but dropped out for lack of funds. Before her marriage she worked as a secretary and editorial assistant at *National Geographic*. After her children were born she started writing short fiction and essays. In Afghanistan she took a correspondence course given by the Newspaper Institute of America. Reading and writing were a central part of her life.[47]]

Letter: January 29, 1952

In a sense, perhaps this is the most momentous letter I have yet written!!! With the help of Osborne's pictures, I have sold an article!!! Last night when Osborne brought in a letter from the National Geographic Society, I opened it and just stared. Looking over my shoulder Osborne broadcast the astounding news that they had sent a check of $1,000 for the pictures and article "Home is Afghanistan". It was the strangest feeling – or lack of feeling. Os took possession of the check and demanded that I decide immediately how it was to be spent but we decided that such an important matter needed a family conclave and we had Amma Ruth's[48] wonderfully long letter and one from Ret to read as well. The children wondered if they might tell the children at school. "We won't brag", Wetherill assured us and we agreed that it would be alright if they didn't mention the check.

It is only now, in telling you that I begin to feel really excited about it! For once I can accept Osborne's "I am proud of you" knowing that it is not just his love but that I have accomplished something fairly passable – of course I have always said that I thought the *Geographic* articles were more notable for their photographs than for their literary quality!! Especially nice is the fact that they have asked for more, since they think I can write another "just as appealing". Thoughts for

47. Her collected writings and other memorabilia are in the "Rebecca S. Cresson Papers" at the Friends Historical Library of Swarthmore College.

48. Since Wetherill and Os had two aunt's named Ruth, the one who married Uncle Emlen in 1949 was named with the Farsi word for aunt: Amma Ruth.

a new article were churning around in my brain and I had only two hours sleep last night, but I guess I have a little something extra to go on, today!

Letter: January 29, 1952

Dick and Mary Ann Irvine were very sweet about the article and Dick said that I might write my next one in the library. I had to laugh afterward when I spent the whole afternoon dashing wildly around helping youngsters find reference material before the next bell rang.

I had given up the idea of doing any more writing because I don't see just when it could be worked in, but the challenge of the *Geographic's* request is intriguing. Tonight Carol and Bob Bucher, Mary Harvey (a nurse from Tabriz) and the three Mullers (Arthur, Beth and Mother) are going to have dinner with us to celebrate. None of us is going to be fit for a very late session and I dropped a hint that it would be acceptably polite for everyone to eat and run!

Osborne has been pulling the check out of his pocket to look at it every so often. After our guests leave I'll take a good look again – after all I may never see another like it! And sometime I hope to have time to get the manuscript out and see how it reads.

Letter: February 4, 1952

We haven't had a chance to all get together on the subject of the check but there seems to be general agreement on bare outlines. First, that half is coming to you, Ret, and secondly, that if we can arrange to get away we will try to meet you in Italy or Switzerland for a couple of weeks this summer!! We feel that we should take the opportunity if we can since you never know what may happen next. I told Osborne that if we put the money in the bank no telling what might happen to it but if we had the trip, there it would be in our memories forever and the next year on the way back to the states we will hope to be able to see France and England. So, begin collecting travel folders and find out how we can do the most on the least and let's do it. If Tiddo could join us wouldn't that be royal!

Letter: June 24, 1952

NatGeoSoc sent a cable for the last picture legends which sounds as though they are getting ready to send the Afghan article to press. Someone intimated that it might come out toward the end of the summer. We aren't getting along very well on the new article. I have some notes but must dig up more historical background for this one. That is something I just haven't energy to do yet.

Letter: November 19, 1952

Life was further complicated by a cable from *National Geographic* asking for another article in a hurry. It was written in three days, pictures assembled and the works off in a week. No answer yet but I keep thinking of how I wish I had written things differently!

Letter: December 29, 1952

You guessed right about the Iran article. I have to do it over to put more of us into it! But they are still willing to be interested. I wish they would publish the first – I'm tired of being asked when it will be.

Letter: December 30, 1952

Os asked in wonder if every article took as much work and decided that editing might be a worthwhile possibility for him in the future. I was interested in the implication that he considered it only after he began to think that it involved a lot of work!!

[Rebecca submitted a revised draft of the Iran article in April, 1953. It was accepted 11 days before we left Tehran, but they asked for more revisions. The magazine was intent on publishing soon to capitalize on interest generated by the increasing disorder in Iran, that ultimately led to the Shah's abdication and quick return to power in August of that year. The Afghan article was published in September and the one on Iran in November. The editors had added "turbulent," "strife-torn" and "troubled" to her title, subtitle and first sentence. Rebecca was upset about the editing but she had no practical way to resist the changes. The excerpts quoted here are from her original manuscript.]

Chapter 12: A Busy Schedule

Letter: July 22, 1951

We spend about 6 hours a week on Farsi and have attended some of the Annual Meeting sessions. Were especially interested in Personnel reports since our housing depended on that. Osborne has been getting in a lot of tennis (at 5:30 A.M.) and is getting into good enough shape so that he is usually on the winning side! Wetherill and Os swim and this morning Os was in a Sunday School play. He spoke clearly in a good resonant Cresson voice. The Cubs had a hike again yesterday.

Letter: June 29, 1951

I feel quite like a suburban housewife in the sense that I taxi children around to innumerable dates – for I am more or less free and most other mothers of the Mission are perpetually busy. My turn will come later and I have already done enough studying of third grade work to get the "feel".

Letter: August 9, 1951

Yesterday the children hauled in two other children for lunch, Tom McNair came for a bite of supper on the spur of the moment and an Iranian, who twice happened upon us when we were struggling with Farsi, came to see us. He will come to dinner next week. On the same day that Navart, a dwarf who is not as tall as Os, is going to help me shop for curtain, slip cover and pajama materials.

Laugh at me if you wish – my sense of duty as Acting Principal's wife pushed me into joining the International Women's Club! Me a woman's club member – whew. At least it will be relieved by such a variety of nationalities represented and I shall have a neutral meeting ground with many of our students' mothers.

Letter: August 23, 1951

The women have decided to have meetings, hereafter, in the morning so I will not go anymore but it was fun that one time. I knew a number of the diplomatic wives there, had a message from Kabul for the wife of the Indian Chargé d'Affaires, and saw the Indonesian Ambassador's wife who was in Kabul last year and who has invited us to their Independence Day party.

But the event of the day was the spectacle that Mrs. Grady made of herself. I didn't dare look around much because the expressions on the faces of especially the American women convulsed me. Mrs. G. was in white watered taffeta – a tailored suite bound in black, fitting her barrel figure as tightly as the seams would allow. She is very short with spindly legs and very thick makeup. On her head she wore a gray veil with two huge cabbage roses (artificial) over one ear. She started out by saying she would not make a speech, a remark that evidently prefaces all her harangues. Then she held forth most of an hour saying that she gave her heart here and there and every old place – it was quite a spectacle.

Letter: September 16, 1951

Wednesday was the first day of school and what excitement in our house. We had four children, three mothers and one father plus two single teachers and we got to school in time anyway! I had to take the roll and conduct the fourth grade over to the church for chapel – the little lambs did just as they were asked to do – except a mishie child!!! Dick Irvine was quite nervous but had a very good short program planned. My library is the saddest looking place you ever saw – when the USIE librarians came in to make suggestions I whipped around the door so fast I saw their unveiled expressions and they were duplicates of just what I felt when I first saw the place. When I told them that, they broke down and suggested that I start by throwing away a good many of the books. The first to go will be one I discovered called *Exercises for Boys and Girls* – printed in 1897!!!

Letter: December 2, 1951

This morning I told Osborne that I thought it would be a quieter week but by noon we had engagements for every day except Friday! Monday to show the doctor our vaccinations, station meeting, Stu Ronald for dinner and a theatrical afterward! Tuesday Osborne has a committee meeting here (they said they would come here because they knew we would feed them!) Wednesday a new English family is coming to tea, Thursday we have a square dance to chaperone and Saturday a dinner at the Buchers to meet a young Quaker who has joined Near East Foundation's farm demonstration group.[49]

Yesterday was a humdinger. I tore around the house getting ready for an Embassy (ex-Mission) family who were coming to spend part of the night before leaving for USA. Went to the library, and Dick asked me to take notes of the noon teachers' meeting (and then the rascal asked me to give a resume of my notes to the meeting – I had to do some hasty filling in!) Mrs. Young came to lunch since there wasn't time for her to go home. At 4:30 when I closed the library Mary Ann, Osborne and I went to Endies' house (Secretary to the Mission Secretary) for tea to meet a Kermanshah nurse, and home to have dinner with our house guests and entertain several who came to say goodbye to them.

49. The Near East Foundation still does grassroots development in the Middle East and Africa. (www.neareast.org)

Chapter 13: Entertaining

Letter: October 2, 1951

We had a gay old time yesterday. After station meeting there was to be a picnic supper at the barbecue between our house and the Elders' where Art Muller and his family are living. Unprecedentedly we had rain and were afraid there was more to come so we moved two long picnic tables into the front hall, put more tables on the porch for the children and managed to seat 42 people. Our four children had worked up a revised version of Tom Sawyer and after supper they opened the doors between the playroom and the dining room and had an ideal stage. It wasn't a perfect performance but had enough vim and vigor to overshadow the rough spots and was so generously applauded that I think it will produce a rash of theatricals. Shades of my youth!! Someone mentioned that it was so nice that we had enough youngsters just in the one family to be able to do such things. In spite of discipline problems I am convinced that my idea of twelve children would have been interesting.

Letter: November 12, 1951

Yeksabet was a gem and made all the food for the party herself – date-filled cookies, walnut cookies, pumpkin tarts made with squash, bread and butter spread very thin with caviar, *nawn* spread with cheese and topped with a thin slice of cucumber, and pierogi [dumplings] which were the only flop. Yeksabet insisted upon making them her way and they weren't the same kind that I thought of.

We had invited over 70 people knowing that with so many busy people a large number would not be able to come. About three-quarters of them came and when things calmed down enough for me to evaluate it I found groups all around talking furiously and seeming frightfully interested in each other. We were able to bring together some of the locally hired teachers (mostly Embassy and Point Four) and the missionaries whom they have had no occasion to meet before, as well as parents from various Embassies.

When people told us that they had thoroughly enjoyed themselves we could believe them. We almost had to push people out because they stayed until it was practically time for the school square dance to begin. Since we chaperone Saturday evening entertainments we had to be there. It was a good dance and though it ended a very full day, we came home and talked until midnight with the caller who is with the film unit out here. That day we had had our regular duties of course, a teachers' meeting, a Scout meeting, a Farsi lesson, a tea and a dance! We weren't idle.

Letter: January 6, 1952

When we left [the mission Christmas party] Osborne and I agreed that it was about time for us to get outside our own little circle for some refreshing ideas – and we got them only I am not sure that we felt them very refreshing. The next evening we had dinner with one of our part-time teachers whose husband is an army man and frankly admitted he was here in Iran only because he didn't want to go to Korea. He can't say enough against the natives or anyone not his own countryman and Osborne and Dick had a hard time restraining themselves. I chose to talk knitting instead of international items and that shows how violently opposed we were! The other guests were a Greek couple who are now American citizens, and we want to see more of them for they have a nice attitude toward world problems – he is a dairy expert with Point Four.

Letter: February 13, 1952

Tuesday we had Mr. and Mrs. Ziyal who are at the Turkish Embassy for dinner with Altay. Ezmari knew Ur Ziyal at Pearl Campbell's school in Kabul. The children arranged the seating – putting Altay where Os could be on one side and Wetherill could be on the other. He lived up to their expectations and kept them entertained during the whole meal. Mr. Ziyal, who has an attractive sense of humor though he is a bland appearing person, was very much interested in our saying the blessing before the meal. He told us they say theirs after the meal. I asked if they omitted the blessing if the food was not good. At the end of the meal he said, "Now I should say a blessing for the food was very good!" There was such a lively twinkle in his small black eyes!

Letter: June 24, 1952

The day before my malaria chills began we went to a station meeting and a station party for the June birthday people. Then Osborne and I skipped off to the Iranian-American Society's final program for the season featuring Fulbrighters[50] and the American Ambassador. There we met a young Iranian couple, Shamaz and Mohamed Hadi Sharifzadeh, who have been back from the U.S. just a few months. They had a wonderful time up near Rochester and named their American born daughter "Virginia" – for Virginia Dare they explained, and me with my low mind thought of the brand of wine instead of the Jamestown baby!!

They asked us to attend Virginia's first birthday party, so we went last night. It was typically Iranian and we were the only Americans. When we entered, the courtyard was lit with electric lights. There were two facing rows of chairs and a table groaning with cakes, fruits and cucumbers at the end. Each guest chose a chair and in that you sat until you left. When honored guests arrived everyone stood up and hands were shaken all around. We found one lady who spoke English and had a nice time visiting with her – she knew and loved the Dreyfuses.[51] They served thick fruit syrup with gin in it. (Osborne claimed he drained his just to find out whether it really was gin!) Then came cups of tea, then cakes and finally the birthday cake – a fruit and whipped cream topped confection with one candle. After a little more conversation with our neighbors on either side and smiles at those opposite us, Osborne and I made our adieux and the host walked up the street with us until we found a taxi.

Letter: August 16, 1952

Today we were just getting up from siestas (required in Tehran) when Stu Ronald, who is eating with us now, brought word that we had a caller. He proved to be Kay Beach, one of Friends Service's agriculturalists who has been in China, India, Pakistan and Afghanistan.[52]

50. The Fulbright Program of the U.S. State Department sent scholars abroad to do teaching and research.

51. Louis and Grace Dreyfus were friends from Kabul where he was the U.S. ambassador, 1949-1951.

52. Kay Haines Beach (1907-1989), of Edwardsville KS, worked for AFSC in re-

We have taken him in to our hostel. It makes us eleven – twelve at table – but gives us a chance to hear more of his experiences. And we know that Friends Service people don't have much money.

Last night Kay showed Wetherill how to do Gujarati embroidery and Janet said that when she woke up he and Wetherill were sitting on the latter's bed in their p.j.s continuing the lesson this morning. Wetherill is planning to make Ret a table cloth with her new embroidery.[53]

We are leaving all our guests to their own devices and to make their own departures after we get off for Hamadan, which is most irregular but quite typical of us I guess!

Letter: February 17, 1953

Our days have been chock-a-block. Dinner was a huge success with the Elders, Chuck Swan and John Howison (who was in the Kabul Embassy when we first arrived). John had a bad introduction to the Mission the first time he attended church – some people have a habit of saying the wrong thing and John was one of the victims and has not come back. We told him we wanted him to know John and Ruth because they are different.

Osborne thought during dinner that we might have trouble getting off trivialities but little John Howison knew what he wanted out of the evening and as soon as we finished coffee in the living room he plunged in with a question. We were terribly proud of John Elder. He took a deep breath and then launched into a concise, well organized reply that led to an evening of extremely thoughtful discussion. Everyone had a good time, I think, and John started attending church again! So Osborne and I accomplished both our purposes – a fund of

building war torn areas. He sounds remarkably like Rebecca and Osborne in a letter about the source of his concern: "My basic reason for being here is a hope that my work may some way serve as a message of good will, and will in at least a small way help the cause of friendship between nations, and render another war a little less likely." (*Friends Bulletin – Pacific Coast Association,* June 1947)

53. Kay learned the Gujarati stitch in India as a gift for his sister, Mary Alta Beach, in the U.S. About 25 years later, Wetherill taught the skill to Rebecca who was living in Costa Rica at the time. Then Rebecca passed it on to women in a local crafts cooperative who were making embroidered clothing for sale to tourists.

thoughtful information and a most pleasant mission contact on one side and a mighty fine example of our diplomatic representatives on the other.

Chapter 14: A Wedding

Letter: June 21, 1951

The tiny music teacher will be changing her name if not her job sometime this summer or fall. Eleanor Engeman, who lives with us and is teaching piano to Wetherill, and Tom McNair, who is head of the Alborz Foundation's adult education, have kept the mission station on pins for they did not declare their intentions soon enough to suit quite a number! Fortunately they are two very nice young people and everyone approves. We have had a chance to know Tom pretty well for we have breakfasts and lunches with him and his assistant, Stu Ronald.

Letter: August 23, 1951

Eleanor will continue giving Wetherill piano lessons even after she is married and no longer living with us. The rest of the family practice, too, and Wetherill has been helping me catch up to where she has gotten to. We are using the Thompson method books and they are very nice, giving real tunes from the very beginning. Os thought it was too bad I couldn't remember how to sing the Volga Boatman in Russian when I was playing a simplified version of it. Busy as I have been and tired, too, it has still been a temptation at 11 PM to practice on the piano!

Rick Pond and Chuck Swan (two young teachers) left their record player with us last night while they went on vacation. We played Brahms' Sonata for Clarinet and pretty soon tiny, blond Eleanor was sneaking down stairs in her wrapper to listen, too. She said she couldn't sleep and it was just the thing she needed – her wedding announcements had just come and she was all keyed up. She is addressing them today.

We are going to share Tom and Eleanor's wedding rehearsal party with the two proxy parents, Mark and Ruth Irwin and Bob and Carol Bucher. I've helped Eleanor put the wedding dress together and shall probably do the hem for she isn't going to get to it herself, I fear. Her mother had done the bodice and left it for Eleanor to finish and fit properly.

Tom and Eleanor gave all the men Persian silk ties and the girls a silver coffee-spoon each. I finished the wedding dress that day and spent most of Friday dashing around receiving gifts, fixing flowers and getting our clothes into shape. We had just what Eleanor wanted for breakfast – bacon and muffins, *lavash* and peaches for cereal. I fixed a white aster corsage which Eleanor wore during the day. She had a nap after lunch and then by 4 PM the family were dressed; Vera Dulaney, the bridesmaid, was dressing in Wetherill's room; Ruth Irwin was pressing the wedding dress, and Eleanor had wakened. It was fun to help her dress and she looked "delectable" in a sweet lace dress with a two-tier finger-tip length veil and Mary Stuart cap of lace. Her bouquet was a tuberose sheaf. Vera wore blue and carried pink and white glads. Osborne was one of the two tenors in the choir and Eleanor planned for the children and me to sit in her "family pew" with Ruth Irwin who acted as bride's mother.

We sent the servants over to the church, locked the front door, and gave the key to Mark Irwin because I knew that I might get stuck and the newlyweds were coming to our house to sign their papers.

The wedding went perfectly, which was a minor miracle because the rehearsal was "clabbered", as Eleanor called it. It was a long affair with 40 minutes of music beforehand and a song, "Wedding Prayer," which Stu did very well in the middle of the service. The best man was an Iranian. Tom looked awfully rigid until Eleanor came smilingly into view. She wasn't at all nervous. The whole thing was quite impressive and since many people who were not Christians came, it was nice to have such a lovely example of a wedding ceremony.

When the service was over Mark was lost and the wedding party went in via the back door. Batool said that was a good beginning and augured well for the marriage! Then a fuse blew out so the papers were signed by kerosene light! They went back to the church to take some pictures and afterward part of the choir and the principals came here for soup, sandwiches and iced tea before the reception. It was a gay gathering, mostly of young people.

The reception was two hours later – a novel arrangement – and at the other compound. The basketball court, out of doors, had carpets, tables, and a 3-tier cake, tea-tables and a piano. I was scheduled to pour at the table nearest the receiving line so I did a hurried business during my stint, which was the early one when the big rush came.

Os went thru the receiving line, kissed the bride, wiped off his mouth, kissed her again and wiped his mouth again – he didn't want any telltale lipstick! Wetherill thoroughly enjoyed the whole business but Os decided that when he marries he will have just the preacher and the bride. I told him that he would have to have two witnesses in America, or four here, so he decided he would have to be married in America to keep it to a minimum.

Chapter 15: Square Dancing

Letter: September 8, 1951

Had a wonderful first evening of square dancing in our living room – a set full of enthusiasts, just to start with.

Letter: October 2, 1951

The mission was well represented in a demonstration square dance at the Iran- America Society[54] – four of us were chosen out of eight. It was fun and now I hear that the school youngsters want a square dance on Saturday. I hope we can get the very good caller we had for the demonstration.

Letter: February 3, 1953

The enthusiasm continues for square dancing and we are gradually acquiring some new followers. Zorick came last week and I was terribly interested to see what a carry-over there is in music. So often I have tried to explain a swing to a man and had to demonstrate time and again before he got the feel of it. I explained the theory to Zorick and before we had completed a full turn he had caught the rhythm and ever after he had it! I think it was mostly due to his perfect sense of timing.

Letter: April 13, 1953

Six new children arrived in school on one day. They are Americans and most of their families are coming to church – and several of them are coming to our square dances which are really going along famously. Osborne is the one who can dance every dance and still have pep enough to ask for more – there were four high school youngsters last Saturday and their eyes almost dropped out.

54. The Iran-America Society promoted cultural exchange and language classes. Their offices were bombed in 1978 and their director was one of the hostages held at the U.S. Embassy for over a year.

Chapter 16: Quaker Meeting

[After marrying in an Episcopal service in Washington DC on January 1, 1937, Rebecca and Osborne searched for a religious home for their new family. They attended Quaker meetings in Washington DC and Syracuse NY and loved it. While living in Putney VT they took their questions about Quakerism to a neighbor who was a Friend. He would listen carefully and then say, "That is up to thee, Osborne (or Rebecca)". They understood he meant we can each be seekers, and supporters of others who are seeking.

As I grew up from the age of 3 in New Mexico to 14 in Arizona, the Quaker meetings we attended were in homes, our own and those of people we knew. This was typical of Rebecca and Osborne's focus on life as a relation among friends, and of their habit of living in out-of-the-way places.]

Letter: August 6, 1950

Osborne wasn't too sure at first that he would want to tie up to the Presbey Board,[55] though Dr. and Mrs. Elder said they would be pleased to have us at Community School in Tehran even though we stayed Quakers as we would insist upon doing.

Letter: April 28, 1951

We won't be asked to do evangelical work and the school is broad minded enough to employ even non-Christian teachers.

Letters: January 6, 1952; January 14, 1952

We have started having a Quiet Hour of meditation on Fridays at our house. Miss Aiden, the half-Iranian British missionary, suggested it to me and the Zoradnicks are pleased to join us. (John is a Quaker working for the Near East Foundation and he and Miriam are former Friends Service Work Campers in Finland.)

We hesitate to do anything which makes our different faith obvious to the Mission but felt the need for time to do our own thinking. Each time some of the missionaries have joined us and we feel that

55. The Presbyterian Board of Foreign Missions hired the Community School staff.

it is filling a great need in our own lives which are so rushed that we don't seem to have time to sort out our values.

We Went to School in Tehran

One day Osborne lit the stove just before the group gathered. As we sat in silent meditation the stove became vocal. It roared and hissed and bellowed. It shook and rumbled ominously. The stovepipe became red-hot and the lid rattled. The air was filled with the noise and threat of our heater. Those who sat with us, though they were Baha'i, Jew, Anglican and Presbyterian, remained resolutely silent and only the lady nearest the stove moved a trifle. The stove, routed perhaps by the determined silence, though more likely by the exhaustion of its surplus fuel, settled more quietly to its business and our meeting continued without comment.

Letter: June 24, 1952

Yesterday a little negro girl who had been with Friends Units in China and India had lunch with us. We were particularly interested in her remark that China is China in spite of the Communists – that the people accept the good they can get out of the new regime and remain essentially themselves throughout. The propaganda they are given seems to be mostly anti-American and no Marxist theory whatsoever. She was so interesting and we were very happy that she got in touch with us. She said that Chester and Julia Bowles were doing a grand job [in the U.S. Embassy] at Delhi. Mrs. Bowles evidently takes an active part in relief and rehabilitation in India.

Letter: October 19, 1952

The Zoradnick baby arrived last night, a boy. All the Near East Foundation people seem to be having boys. There is going to be another Quaker baby in February, so our circle is growing. We now have five more regular attenders at Friday Quiet Time.[56] Beverly and John

56. Quiet Time was our name for the Quaker meeting in our living room on Friday mornings. It was also something we did occasionally simply to settle down. Also, when buses stopped and men got out to pray, we held our own Quiet Time.

Macauley and Luanna Bowles are from our home meeting,[57] no less. Luanna had dinner with us this week and what an interesting person she is! She had been in Japan setting up new educational standards during the occupation and is helping on education here, in Point Four.

Letter: May 27, 1953

Both Margies [Frame and Gurney] and Wetherill went on a scout hike today. The rest of us had Quiet Time on the porch overlooking our pleasant garden with delphinium in a riot of bloom.

57. Our home meeting was Friends Meeting of Washington D.C., sometimes called Florida Avenue Meeting. When Rebecca and Osborne became Friends in about 1939, they lived in Putney, VT. There was no meeting near them and so Florida Avenue Meeting accepted us into membership. (Rebecca lived in Washington DC before they married there in the Episcopal Cathedral there on January 1, 1937.)

Chapter 17: The Presbyterian Mission

Missionaries:

Letter: June 29, 1951

There is something mighty kindly and friendly about these Mission people. They have welcomed us just as tho we were good Presbyterians and most of them don't know that that is the way I started out!

Letter: June 29, 1951

You might be interested to hear what keeps these folks busy. Mrs. Elder, among her regular church duties, has started an employment agency and what a horde of people she has from seven until five on her Agency days. Mrs. Payne works at a clinic in South Teheran, Mrs. Bucher teaches illiterates and Miss Chase teaches sewing and excellent embroidery. Miss Doolittle has an informal school which takes privileged girls in the mornings and under-privileged girls in the afternoons, for reading, cooking, Bible and handwork. Mrs. Port doesn't do very much away from home but has been hostess for the Albers students – adult classes in English, music, Bible, etc.

Letters: June 21, 1951, June 29, 1951

Introducing the mission community, first in our affections are the Elders who have the sweetest dispositions and the love of all the Mission and the Iranians as well. Dr. Elder's chief job is publications but he is on just about every committee going. He has a rare quiet sense of humor. Mrs. Elder is in charge of women's activities. Along with her regular church duties, she has started an employment agency and what a horde of people she has from 7 until 5 on her agency days.

Letter: July 23, 1951

Ruth Elder makes us all seem like such pokes! She directs the gardeners, assists Property Committee, entertains everyone who comes around, has been taking care of mid-morning snacks for Annual Meeting, plays for weddings, funerals and Farsi church services, runs a small children's library and an employment agency, rents equipment to newly arrived Americans and still has time to answer each question the children may ask. And I have had trouble getting down to making Wetherill's dresses! Of course I've been going to parts of Annual Meeting, studying Farsi and Educational Methods, helping Wetherill and Os finish the tag ends of lessons, and mending innumerable socks.

Letter: February 3, 1953

John Elder is doing the services for the English-speaking congregation now and there is a different feeling – and we notice quite a few new faces. Previously I had begun to develop my ability to concentrate quite well: when the sermon started I would concentrate on my own thoughts and seldom knew much about the sermon at the end of the service, but John is ruining that. He preaches such downright sermons I listen in spite of myself!

Ezmari's Visit:

Letter: October 15, 1951

We had a letter from Ezmari in Kabul addressed to "Dear gentle family" and still hoping to come to see us during winter holiday. How we would like to show him our school![58]

Letter: January 29, 1952

Day before yesterday we had what we thought was exceptional excitement. A telegram arrived from Ezmari who is on his way to visit us!! He, you remember, was the very good friend who traveled to Faizabad with us and who was such a great help in getting us off for Iran. We didn't think that he would be able to come but are anxiously awaiting his arrival, any day now. What fun it will be to show him Community School and perhaps we will see some of the interesting things around town that we haven't gotten around to.

Letter: February 13, 1952; The House at 51 Howellville Road

Ezmari has arrived. He went to see the Cochrans in Mashhad and when Bernice met him at the door she said, "Come right in. You

58. Ezmari was one of Osborne's Afghan students who we felt very close to. (See *We Felt Their Kindliness . . .*, Chapter 16: Ezmari, and Chapter 26: Faizabad.)

are going to stay with us." That is so like her and we were so happy about it because there couldn't be better people for him to know.

He brought us a handsome rug in a typical Afghan "elephant's foot" design. He also had good pictures of baby John Popplestone and numerous letters from friends in Kabul. [Typically, Osborne dubbed the baby "Popplepebble".]

Ezmari says that things are not very happy at Habibia College [where Osborne had worked]. People seem dissatisfied but perhaps they are just feeling the effects of the smaller American teaching staff. They have only one course other than English taught by an American.

Ezmari has gone to Community School and the 11th grade has put themselves out to be nice to him. They came looking for him so that he won't miss anything, had him practice basketball with them, urged him to come to a square dance where they encouraged him to dance a reel, and our nice Altay Ziyal took him to the mill station in Shemiran yesterday which was a lovely drive.

It is rather interesting how critical Ezmari is about everything. It's the old Afghan pride, I am sure. Tehran is so much bigger and more modern than Kabul but I hope that we will be able to give him a sense of balance, an appreciation for what is due while still retaining his fondness for his own city. We aren't able to do much to entertain him for we have regular obligations every day until 5 or 6 o'clock, except on Friday!

Letter: March 2, 1952

Osborne went to bed with a fever. When the Embassy nurse found I was running quite a fever she put me to bed, too. Bill Miller took Ezmari to his house so he wouldn't catch it.

[What happened next had difficult consequences because Ezmari became a Christian. Rebecca and Osborne strongly advised him to remain a Muslim so that he could do good work in his home country. Everyone knew that renouncing his Muslim faith would be severely punished by the Afghan government. However, Ezmari was persuaded to smuggle a Bible into Afghanistan and he was jailed soon after his return. His family, who loved him, had to disown him. He finally got out of Afghanistan and made his way to Europe and then to Africa where there is credible evidence that he created problems for himself and others and died while still young.

Rebecca was extremely upset by this. In her diary she described two aspects of Bill Miller:]

Diary, March 11-April 12, 1953

Bill Miller – bigoted and relentless in beliefs but with a real Christian humility and kindliness.

[When Rebecca wrote about him to her family, she typically emphasized the positive and only hinted at the negative:]

Letter: April 12, 1953

There are some truly rare souls and Bill Miller is one of them. Bill is what you think of as a typical missionary as far as his mannerisms go but he really tries to live his faith and even had some effect on us! We have always felt that we could talk problems over with him whether he would have our point of view or not. John and Ruth Elder are our other rare souls.

[Rebecca rarely wrote about difficult personal issues but she recorded some incidents in two pages in the back of her diary under the title "Re: Mission".]

Diary: March 11-April 12, 1953

Soghra Hannum (Azimi) said she didn't go to church because the missionaries were such poor examples of what they preached. Clem Scott said he had heard the same story. I heard it from Navart & Haikin as well. John Zoradnick said he stopped coming to church because the first two times he was there the sermons were both rants criticizing other branches of the Christian faith. Art Muller made snide remarks like calling John Howison a "backsliding Methodist" the first time John went to church. He didn't go back until after we introduced him to the Elders.

[The following is from Rebecca's diary two days after we left

Iran in 1953.[59] We were staying with Park and Alice Johnson in Beirut, Lebanon. Park was the Field Representative of the Presbyterian Board of Foreign Missions responsible for mission work in Lebanon, Syria, Iraq and Iran. Alice was a teacher who also worked for the Near East Council of Churches.]

Diary: June 24, 1953

At breakfast Park did some digging for information & we spoke plainly about some of the problems as we saw them in Tehran. We had not expected to talk but Park needs to have some background because he is going over to try to whip Tehran Station into better shape so we broke down & told what we thought.

Dickin:

Letter: April 12, 1953

I am missing John Elder's wonderful sermons but one can't expect a much younger man to have John's ability and Leon Dickinson has other qualities which makes him admirably suited to the English-speaking congregation to which he has been appointed as pastor. He is a Congregationalist, has had several tours as a Navy chaplain and took our breaths away by the facility he has in remembering names. At the reception the Gurneys gave for him John Elder says there was a lull and then Dickin said, "Now let me see how many names I can pin on the people." The room was crowded but he named all but four or five correctly!!! Just having met them as they went thru the receiving line! And he remembers them, too.

He is right there when it comes to getting into activities where he can meet people on their ground. He is coming to the next basketball game and will square dance with us on Saturday. When we invited him to the tea-dance we are giving for the 11th and 12th grades at our house on Thursday, he grabbed at the chance of meeting those youngsters. He joined our discussion group and has gone to scads of Embassy affairs, too, I believe.

He is staying with Henrietta Gurney (of USIE) and she says

59. The diary is published in *We Stood in Awe: Rebecca's Travel Diaries 1949 and 1953*, ed. Os Cresson, Iowa City IA: Morning Walk Press, 2020.

that already women are coming to lean on his broad and good-looking shoulder. She has asked if Yeksabet would take care of him because Henrietta thinks Yeksabet could handle the women! Church is crowded – partly curiosity, partly Easter – and we like the more reverent pace that Dickin sets for the service.

Letter: April 20, 1953

Wetherill helps out when we need an extra woman on square dance nights and even Os can swing his partner as well as some of the men. Our Dickin – the new minister – proved to be very good and promised Jasmin that he would come again. She also got him to promise to come to play games on Friday morning (I am lazy and lie in bed and listen to the young things holler). Dickin said he would be ready to sit down to our Quiet Time after playing games, so maybe he plans to join us.

Letter: May 19, 1953

Osborne had to go to class but Dickin and I had a fine talk – fine, I suppose, because we found ourselves in such pleasant agreement! We covered religion and politics and all kinds of subjects.

Letter: May 27, 1953

After the church supper everyone gathered in the auditorium. We sang, Dickin made a little talk and the square dancers put on a demonstration. Our family danced together in one set representing what fun families can have square dancing together. Osborne had Wetherill as his partner and Os was mine. After the demonstration each of us dragged out someone from the audience for a simple square and the rest of the evening we had three or four squares of interested people. Osborne's comment was "Dickin's done it. There never was a church supper like this before – not <u>here</u>!" and I must say that Dickin seemed to hit the right tone.

Letter: June 18, 1953

In the evening Dickin took us to see his house but we couldn't get in. He came back and had dinner with us and while Osborne corrected papers Dickin threw a parish problem at me. He sometimes does that just to see what my reaction may be and whether it agrees with his. Fortunately I usually do agree!

[The diary Rebecca wrote on the journey back to the U.S. has the following two notes apparently intended for a letter to Dickin:]

Diary: July, 1953

It was in Rome, when we were going from place to place in a sightseeing bus, that Wetherill asked about my father.[60] Did I ever tell you that he was evidently quite a priceless personality? He attached the affection and allegiance of people not only to himself but also to his beliefs, ideals and way of life. Wetherill considered a while, then remarked confidently, "He must have been a wonderful man – just like Uncle Dickin."

Diary: July, 1953

Been jittering about the job ahead [public speaking after returning to the U.S.], wanting to do it well but fearful of inadequacy. This was in a birthday book for March 31st: "Things well done, and with care, exempt themselves from fear." You would have gone on from there wouldn't you? Have you ever done a sermon on that? Would like to see it.[61]

Letter: Spring, 1955

Think I will close my talk to the women's group this afternoon with the Gelasian Sacramentary prayer you printed in the order of service the last Sunday we were in Tehran. Remember it? "Oh Thou, who art the Light of the minds that know Thee..."

[Rebecca probably noticed that the quoted words could describe the special friend she was writing to. She kept in touch with

60. Rebecca's father, Thomas Berry Shannon, was a Presbyterian minister who died of pneumonia when she was 1½ years old.

61. The date she cited was Dickin's birthday. The birthday book, with a Shakespeare quote for each day, was bought in Shakespeare's hometown on our way from Iran to America.

Dickin for the rest of her life and carried a letter from him in her purse when we moved from Monteverde, Costa Rica to Medford Leas Retirement Community in New Jersey in 1997. Dickin died on January 30, 2000 in Pleasant Hill, TN. He was survived by his wife, Phyllis, and three children. (*Hartford Courant,* February 4, 2000.)]

School

Overleaf: *Students arriving at the front door of Community School.*

Community School, when it was in the Central Compound.

A pond at the old school. This is where Os heard a bullet ricochet overhead during a riot outside the compound walls.

The 4th grade class, 1950-51, the year before Wetherill and Os moved to Tehran. Margie is at front and center.

A class picture, with Wetherill passing by on the porch in back.

A student who commuted on his bicycle.

Rev. John Elder greeting church goers in the Central Compound. He was the head of the mission and much respected by Rebecca and Osborne.

The congregation after church.

People flocking out of the church.

The front gate of Community School in the New Compound with Mahmoud, ever vigilant. He was the gatekeeper, telephone operator and translator . . . an important regulator of school life.

Our school bus.

The parking lot, with one of the older boys parked on the sign.

A bilingual sign.

Walking to class.

The front door of the school.

Beginning a school day.

View from the school water tower, basketball court below and Alborz mountains in the distance.

Some of the older students in a classroom. This used to be the hospital Delivery Room, and it is where Margie Hoffman was born!

The 6th grade taking a quiz, Margie at the left front and Os behind her. She still holds her hand like that when concentrating.

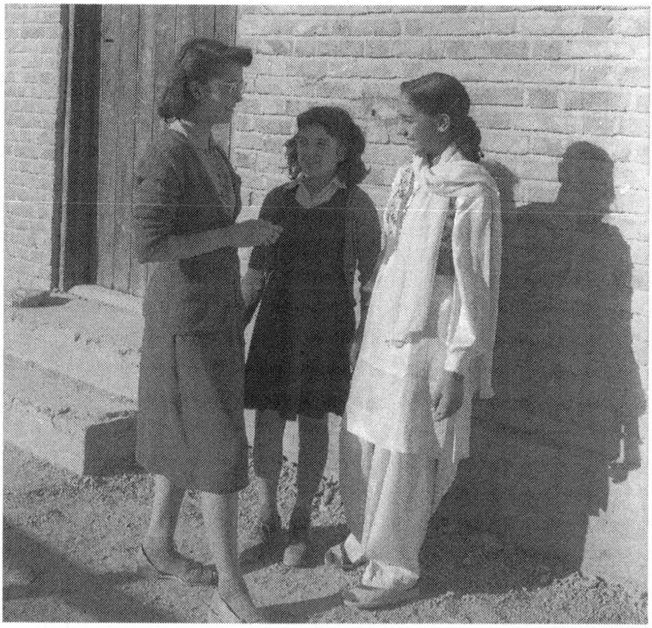

Three of Wetherill's classmates, of Persian, Armenian and Hindu background. The 500 students came from 31 nations.

The mix of cultures in the school, and in Iran; from the left: Isaac was Jewish, Turi was Persian, Nicolas was Russian, and Bella was Armenian. Our home is in the background and that is Rex, one of our two dogs.

Studying the National Geographic, *a valuable window on the world. Rebecca worked for them before she married, and later published two articles in the magazine on our lives in Afghanistan and Iran (Sept. and Nov., 1953).*

The baseball and soccer field at Community School. Os is pitching.

Soccer was big in Iran. The wall was in bounds so you could pass the ball off it. This is where Os' life-long passion for the sport began.

Ping pong under the trees in the school yard.

The ping pong partners facing you were Iraqi and Russian refugees, and the onlooker was French. It was a culturally rich environment.

Community School faculty celebrating the end of the 1952-1953 school year at the barbecue near our home in the New Compound. Chuck Swan is in the center facing the camera.

Osborne and Rebecca with Richard and Mary Ann Irvine and their sons, Mark and David.

Community school faculty. The tall man is Clem Scott, and Chuck Swan is to the right of him.

A celebration at Community School during the 1952-1953 school year.

A celebration at Community School during the 1952-1953 school year.

Richard Irvine, the Community School principal.

The Boy Scouts pledging allegiance.

The school chorus. Anne, Os, Margie and Wetherill are in the front row.

The Girl Scouts. Wetherill is in the front row, fourth from the left.

A Maypole dance.

A square dance.

Doing the Virginia Reel.

A large group practicing the Virginia Reel.

Students pretending to be nurses.

A basketball shooting contest.

A fishing game at a school fair.

Boy Scouts pretending to shoot rifles.

Hot dogs, popular even in Tehran.

The crowd at the school fair.

Chapter 18: The Community School

[Here is a bit of the history of the school that was central in our lives from 1951 to 1953: Community School began providing English language instruction for Presbyterian Mission children in Hamadan in the early 1900s, and moved to Tehran in the 1930s. They soon had about 100 students in ten grades. In 1940 when the Iranian government prohibited instruction in English for Iranian students, Community School stayed open because it served non-Iranian students. With the influx of English-speakers after the war, Community School grew rapidly, and the Ministry of Education began giving permits for Iranian students to attend.]

We Went to School in Tehran
Diary: Notes; Holiday Letter: December 7, 1951

It was almost like being invited to United Nations for Community School had 31 nationalities represented in its student body.[62] The 30 or so teachers used only English in their classes although, like the students, they came from widely varying national and religious backgrounds.

Having been started for mission children, Community School had grown until, in 1952, it offered an American type education to 500 students who could not easily fit into the Iranian school system – American children and those from various Embassies, Iranians who had grown up in the United States or Europe and could not yet read or write their own language, refugees from half a dozen countries, and missionary children. We also had Iranians who had special permission from the Ministry of Education to attend a school run by foreigners. The government wants the Iranian children to go to the government schools but there are quite a few who want what Community School gives – a thorough scholastic training and a high moral standard (that

62. In a note on June 11, 1952, Rebecca listed the following student nationalities: American, Iranian, Iraqi, Greek, Syrian, Indian, Czech, Lebanese, British, Austrian, Hungarian, German, Turkish, Russian, Yugoslav, Dutch, French, Polish, Indonesian, Romanian, Swiss, Danish, Bulgarian, Icelandic, Italian, Nicaraguan, Pakistani, Swedish, Chinese, and Saudi Arabian. Their religions were Christian, Jewish, Muslim, Baha'i, Hindu, Sikh and Zoroastrian.

most recognize as based on Christian). Some were children of government officials, including Premier Mosaddeq's grandniece.

Many of the students spoke four or five languages. One day as I passed the basketball court five boys were practicing baskets. Before I was out of earshot I heard Hebrew, Russian, Armenian, Farsi and English spoken!

Letter: October 15, 1951

A substitute teacher told me today that she couldn't quite put her fourth-grade class together so she inquired a bit about backgrounds and found that out of 31 students there were 14 different languages spoken in the homes! She began to realize that there was little hope of melding them into a unit in a hurry.

Letters: September 16, 1951, October 15, 1951

Some awfully nice youngsters are here and the most appealing are usually the problem children. It is no wonder there are problems with such hectic backgrounds, such as the one who was born in China and escaped, the German refugee children who have grown up in a concentration camp, Czechs who have been told that they must leave Iran and can find no country to receive them, the children of broken international marriages who know no Farsi, poor little army children who have been in 15 schools in seven years, and so many other cases.

Letter: October 21, 1951

This year [1951] we have about 350 students from first to eleventh grade – actually in those eleven years our youngsters do full high school credits for they don't have crafts and some of those nice extras. Each grade has two music and two Bible classes each week and the program is quite well balanced now that Chuck Swan has been given history classes (he expects to get his PhD in History). Next year we will add Physics which couldn't be included this year because of schedules. Dick Irvine is working on preparations for moving into a new building and if we can get the required number of teachers we will have a 12th grade and some of the extras.

Letter: December 4, 1951

I shepherded the last of the students to the clinic for chest ex-rays (for TB) and had one myself. Osborne says that, though the complete reports are not in, there are a number of cases that need investigation, so it may be fortunate we have gone to all this trouble. But best of all we hear that because Community School has had all its students x-rayed, all other schools in Tehran are going to undertake it. If they follow through on positive cases it will be a fine thing to have started.

Holiday Letter: December 7, 1951

Another activity of Osborne and myself is chaperoning weekly dances for the upper school. Sometimes they are social dancing, sometimes square dancing, but always they are most enjoyable because the youngsters behave so nicely. Osborne says that he has not yet seen any ugliness or meanness around school – he has seen mischief, high spirits, and headstrongness of course, but nothing downright bad – and so much that is especially fine.

Letter: October 2, 1951

We have had our first football game (soccer to you) and Os has decided that he will have to play that game. We have two excellent players but Osborne would rather like to smooth out some of their rough spots. Our little Indonesian friend (the Ambassador's son) is goalie and a good one. [The previous school administration] had been all against sports and it is a new regime and indeed seems to have faculty support. The players were quite pleased when our whole family turned out for the game and they didn't know that Osborne had told Dick he ought to appear. It was nice to feel the warmth and friendliness of the spectators and players.

Letter: November 12, 1951

Thursday we had our last soccer game, won 3 – 1 without our star player. The male teachers were all giving a choir concert at Alborz, the adult education center, so that I represented the faculty. While the teams dressed I hung around the school building – and grabbed a stranger when I saw him running down the hall with one of our diminutive janitors chasing him. The boy wrenched loose and I screamed for some of our team who were just leaving to stop him. They ran down the street after him while the janitor told me that he had taken some phonograph records. Then I began to worry about some of our nice boys and went out to find them. They were coming back, having stopped the thief who said that he had dropped the records (the janitor found them, at least some of them). The captain of the opposing team was most apologetic, and said the boy was an outsider, not one of their team. We told him that the team was responsible for whatever happened in the room they occupied.

[Community School remained in operation until the Iranian revolution in 1979. There is an alumni group in the U.S. that have held 11 reunions since 1975. (See: www.csreunion.com)]

Chapter 19: The New School Compound

Letter: June 24, 1952

Today is the day we take official possession of the new compound. I hope work will start soon on reconstruction. We have just employed a new gardener and hope that he will do something with this compound which has good possibilities but has been neglected. There aren't even flowers for the house.

We Went to School in Tehran

Community School took over an old hospital and remade it into a school building. When we moved into a house in the same compound I listened while the masons built their walls. "Listen" is correct for all day long I heard variations on the rhyme [in Farsi]:

One for father
One for mother
One for baby
Hurry up, another.

The bricklayer chanted and at the last word in each line his assistant who stood on the ground, tossed up another brick. At times the bricks were flying up fifteen feet or more. A hod-carrier or lift would have been more efficient but far less entertaining.

A steam shovel and a bulldozer would have speeded construction, too, for all our excavations were done by pick and shovel with the dirt carried out of the hole on a wooden stretcher by two coolies. With their hand tools, day after day coolies worked at leveling the soccer field and remaking the gardens.

Picture Captions

Gulam Hussein, Community School's gardener, was an artist who worked harder than any of his assistants – rather contrary to most supervisors. He was a very able man who not only planned the landscaping and did a large share of the work but even arranged cut flowers so well that I refrained from rearranging them.

The former Mission Hospital was converted into a school building and though there were numerous difficulties and the finer touches are not yet finished, we do have much more attractive quarters than the ancient structure that we occupied last year. Rebecca is particularly pleased with the library which is the old children's ward, a large room with windows on three sides and scads of new books – not new but different, being donations from other libraries. We have a nice auditorium with a stage, footlights, and scenery drops, in which both Middle and Upper School can meet for Chapel and Assemblies. The enrollment is up from 346 to 500 and Osborne is once again teaching without textbooks for those ordered for the newly added twelfth grade have not yet arrived. Osborne has 11th and 12th Math as well as a private office where he counts his money. His accounting has been complicated by all the building operations, moving, equipment etc.

Chapter 20: School Programs

Letter: January 6, 1952

On Tuesday the Middle School had their Christmas program. Os was the announcer for the fifth-grade play and Margie was the cutest looking little doll you could ever hope to see. The seventh grade had members from eight different countries tell of their Christmas customs. Wednesday the Upper School put on its program. Tenth contributed the pianist, ninth had a play written by three American girls, with the characters played by Czech, Arab, Iraqi, Iranian-British and American students. I had worried a bit about their theme – a worthless father who reformed because he caught the Christmas spirit, but they put it over quite well and there was only a little titter when the stage father and mother rushed into a gingerly embrace.

Even more, I had worried about the eleventh-grade skit which was still being written the afternoon before the performance! It had its rough spots but the actors showed considerable poise and the electricians had planned some rather effective lighting. Everyone seemed to enjoy it. We ended up with a most dependable reading by an eighth grader of the Christmas Mouse which was quite amusing. On the whole, I was not too disgruntled at the production my committee had put together in such short order. An eleventh grader was master of ceremonies and the whole thing was pretty much the youngsters' own inspiration, which is as it should be and probably why it went over so well.

Thursday morning the Primary Department put on their show for a roomful of teary-eyed and nervous parents. Mrs. Yavru's first grade did a very good job of a simple little Santa Claus story but the other productions were too ambitious and a bit hectic. It was the afternoon performance and the repetition at night for parents which was the gem. Mary Ann Irvine coached it and showed her ability wonderfully. It was a simple pantomime, artistically staged, with a script written by Chuck Swan and Mary Ann and beautifully read by a bass-voiced tenth grader (an Arabian Jew!) Most of the characters wore our Afghan clothes! The various types of coats were fine for shepherds and wise men and the Madonna looked lovely, swathed in Os' blue turban cloth.

She is an Iraqi with a sweet face, curly black hair and tremendous dark eyes. I had never thought of her as so strikingly beautiful, but with the spotlight on her, the contrast in her coloring and her clear-cut features made a memorable picture. Interspersed throughout the reading was Christmas music sung in four or five languages. Joann Bucher did a solo in a fine-growing soprano. She was a bit nervous in the final performance and didn't hit her high note quite as well as in the afternoon before the student body, but it was a superb production.

Letter: February 13, 1952

There are many activities for Valentine's Day – several class parties, a football game and a big costume dance in the evening. It seems that the youngsters chose Osborne and me as their chaperones at the dance. We are the only faculty members who enjoy dancing ourselves and evidently the youngsters like that. I dance only with Osborne so that the boys don't feel obligated but Osborne dances with the wallflowers and maybe the boys like that, too!

Letter: May 19, 1952

Tenth grade put on a carnival to earn expenses for a party they wish to give the eleventh grade after school closes. One boy rigged up an address system and I could hear his announcements and the dance music, including our dance band, and some of the hubbub. [Rebecca was in bed at home with the mumps.]

A shower wilted the decorations but didn't dampen the spirits of the crowd. It was Osborne's last day at home after the mumps and he wandered over at the end to see how things were winding up. The ice cream had all been sold, most of the pop and sandwiches, the stunts had paid off well and he helped Berry Kashi, the deep-voiced Christmas pantomime reader, usher the horses and donkeys out of the back gate. Berry had been in charge of the rides around the football field and had missed the rest of the activities. He told Osborne that he was anxious to see how things were going and limped way as fast as his aching arches would take him. Berry is quite heavy and couldn't count how many circuits he had made walking the animals around the field!

Letter: May 19, 1952

One nice activity which they used last year and expect to make a permanent feature was a United Nations pledge, repeated in the language of each nation represented in the school: "I pledge allegiance to my country and to the United Nations of which it is a part. One world brotherhood of peaceful nations with liberty and justice for all."[63]

Just as the Thursday performance was to start, the young Embassy mother who had directed the chorus rushed up and told Mary Ann Irvine that an Under-Secretary of State had arrived and she had to put in an appearance. She asked Mary Ann to take over the chorus – they knew the songs and there wouldn't be any hitch. She didn't know that Mrs. Yavru, who was supposed to accompany them, was tied up on some emergency. When Mary Ann sat down at the piano ready to start she discovered that the music she had consisted of just one note! She struck a chord and the chorus was off with Mary Ann filling in around them!!! Half way through she leaned over to the nearest child to find out how many verses they sang and I bet not a soul knew what a predicament she was in. That gal has what it takes.

On Friday a mixed square of teachers and pupils did a dance that brought tremendous applause and Osborne said it was excellently done.

Letter: June 24, 1952

The night after Commencement was the 10th grade's party for the 11th which was really something. One of the Embassy parents arranged for it to be held at the Officers' Club where we had the roof to ourselves with the orchestra from the Park Hotel, the best in town, and a very good dinner with corsages for Mary Ann, Betty Carr and me. Osborne and I danced almost every dance and one of the orchestra men even complimented us on our polka! He is an Italian trumpet player and promised to visit us which the children hope he will do – plus trumpet!

63. Rebecca and Osborne were strong supporters of the U.N. Their mutual interest in peace and international cooperation was part of what drew them to each other in their first conversations after meeting onboard the "S. S. Haiti" in September, 1935.

Letter: November 19, 1952

The Halloween holiday was something. Osborne said he thought it was more important here than in America. All the classes had parties starting with the Primary parade of costumes around the compound. In the evening the sixth grade held a party in their room, which their young teacher handled very well, and the eighth-grade party was in the auditorium. I shuttled between the two, Osborne helped the sixth graders square dance and all our four children were invited to that. It was over an hour before the 8th grade's party so our smallest children went to bed and Wetherill stayed to have a dance with Osborne. She had a terrific rush for there were more 8th grade boys than girls. Everyone thought it such fun that they decided to have regular dances for the Middle School and appointed Wetherill chairman. She has been quite efficient and has it all arranged for tomorrow as a start. Chuck has teased her because the Upper School planned a dance for the same time, put up posters and everything, without finding out whether the auditorium would be free. Fortunately for the younger ones their request was all in order and they must win out but the upper grades are going to be peeved. They have the idea that they come first in all activities and it is going to be a jolt.

Letter: February 17, 1953

This past week was a humdinger – the Valentine Saint took over the place. Preparations were frantic for the two parties on Thursday – Osborne and I were asked to chaperone both! When we first went over there were only boys at the High School party in the auditorium but the girls finally got themselves dressed and quite an original bunch they turned out to be. There was a girl afloat with balloons, one with a solid dress of popcorn, several in saris, two Roman matrons and one Caesar – which I claimed was taking their course in Roman History pretty seriously. I would have given one of the Roman ladies the prize for the prettiest but a girl who had made her own costume as Marie Antoinette won – she had done a good job and her features even looked surprisingly like pictures I have seen. The street cleaner with "Yankee Go Home" printed on his shirt was the big surprise of the evening. He is a proper little Jewish boy who complains if his math mark is below 99 and has never before this year taken any interest in school activities. We were quite content that he got the prize for the funniest though his friend as a beggar did a crack-up dramatic job of his role. The little eighth graders peeked at the high school festivities and felt rather let down with their own party. It was not well planned and didn't seem so gay so Osborne and I spent all our time there when other grownups arrived at the High School party.

Letter: May 27, 1953

Parents Day (or Days) was the big event of last week. The first day was for Nursery thru 6th and the second day 7th thru 12th so that we were represented both days. The smaller group was colorful and the little tikes were so cute and well trained. The usual pledge of allegiance to the United Nations in the language of each country represented in school was an inspiring note each day. By counting Armenian, which Osborne thought we should not do since it is not a country now, we had 32 national languages. The last event of the first day was the humdinger for Osborne and me. There were three groups dancing the Texas Star and Os was the caller! He stood up there in a straw hat and his glasses and went about it like a professional. His hands showed that he was nervous but his voice was as smooth and drawling as though he were talking to himself instead of before a several hundred people. Coming over the mike his voice sounded surprisingly mature.

The second day, seventh grade did a choral program in French, Czech and English as their contribution and the high school put on some amusing skits representing their courses. We thought things went off very well and lots of parents came. Seventh grade received much commendation for their Social Science display. Boys had made model farms, mosques and buildings while the girls made dolls representing the various countries and peoples they had studied. Wetherill's contribution was a two-foot doll with a papier-mâché face which she modeled herself. He was a Pueblo Indian and I hear that one parent exclaimed, "Why he looks just like one!" Wetherill points out that his proportions aren't quite right but he certainly is effective and his face has the proper cast. She calls him "Marcus" after our good Santa Clara friend, Marcus Silva.[64]

64. Marcus Silva was a special friend when we lived in Española, NM. He was an artist and a craftsman and he helped us get to know the Pueblo Indians. He built a large wooden box, about 3 feet on a side, to help ship our household goods to Afghanistan. In Kabul we disassembled the boards to make book shelves. They were put back together as "Marcus' Box" for the move to Tehran, then became shelves again, and finally ended as a battered old box that accompanied us to Arizona, Philadelphia and Iowa.

Chapter 21: Osborne's Work

Letter: June 21, 1951

Fortunately, Richard Irvine, the missionary assigned as superintendent of Community School, will get here in August so that Osborne will be able to duck all the teacher schedule problems and, when we know where the school will be operating next term, spend July getting the plant ready to run. Osborne is to be business manager and assistant super. Frankie Fisher[65] told me that her husband was thrilled at Osborne's ability and attitude and felt that he had everything needed for the job!

Letter: September 16, 1951

Sunday we spent preparing the last lists and plans for the coming entrance examinations. Tom and Eleanor McNair were here for supper and by Monday morning we were ready for the fray. That day was for re-examination of conditional students. It went in quite an orderly fashion with only one irate parent who changed her story two or three times and finally ended up by doing exactly what Osborne and Dick Irvine had decided should be done. One boy who was removed from the list because he had refused to do the academic work brought his father and uncle to plead for him. Osborne refused them until Dick walked into the office and then they tackled him. Dick said when he looked up at the perspiring father who towered and hulked over him, he wondered just what the outcome of it might be!

Exams were over by lunchtime and we worked all afternoon preparing for examination of new students on Tuesday. Our teatime was an informal faculty meeting and by midnight all ends were tied. The next day was of the nightmare variety. At quarter to eight we pushed through the horde of applicants to get to the office door. Steve, the invaluable young Czech refugee secretary, was posted at Dick's desk to take registrations and fees for the exam. Dick and Osborne stood by to help on difficult problems and I was posted at the door to keep people out. They were apt to crowd in like a subway jam. We decided to have them line up and the little Armenian math teacher said that

65. Frankie was the wife of the previous principal of Community School.

she would stand outside to direct because she could speak Farsi. At one point she called to me – all I could see were her large almond shaped eyes wide in desperation – so I plowed through to her. "I can't do anything with them" she gasped. When the people nearest overheard they good naturedly backed off and helped keep better order until Osborne went down the hall and told people to mind their manners.

Letter: October 21, 1951

Both Dick and Osborne are glad to be teaching a few courses because they are in closer touch with the students and with what is going on. Osborne says he picks up a good bit of gossip that way and we get more through our youngsters – we should have one of our family in every class!

Holiday Letter: December 7, 1951

Osborne likes his math classes where students really study and are quick to understand. He is also singing in the church choir and getting extra jobs of accounting for various mission enterprises.

Christmas Card, 1951

As long as I'm bragging (just to you) – Carol Bucher says that many people are making remarks about Osborne's fine teaching – Carol's own Joann is a prime example. On the verge of failing geometry for three months, with Osborne's patient guidance she finally began to see the light and pulled two 90s in tests this past fortnight!

Letter: December 30, 1952

Osborne has been working on closing the books and Os had great fun adding up the figures on an abacus he received in his stocking. Osborne has used one since he has no adding machine but Os had never used one before and found it quite intriguing. He was elated when he added a column faster than Osborne could do it in his head. They both got the same answer, too!

Letter: March 7, 1953

Osborne's classes have fun trying him out and how they applaud when they find they can't stump him! One of the girls who was a problem last year has been working hard and after Osborne had drawn a smiling face on one of her good papers she prepared the way for him by drawing a blank face each time. She has been working like everything to have smiling faces! And she thinks Osborne is wonderful.

Letter: April 13, 1953

After Sunday church service we held a regular dating session and came away with our date book crammed for the whole week. Osborne hasn't had time to think yet that all these dates aren't going to give him much time for marking papers – don't believe I'll mention it for he will become aware of it soon enough. He is so daggone conscientious about it that he tries always to give back all papers within 24 hours. Sometimes it is hard on him.

[Osborne loved teaching about the world and how it operates. One sunny morning in Hamadan, walking along a lane lined by thistles, Dad suddenly launched into a story about sithles and thistles. Sithles didn't have spines like thistles. The cows ate the sithles before they produced seeds but the thistles they didn't eat had seeds and that is why today there aren't any sithles but there are lots of thistles. It was amazing to me how this simple process works to make the world we see around us, and how much fun it was learning about it, and how beautiful it all was.]

Chapter 22: Rebecca's Work

Letter: June 21, 1951

It looks as though I am pretty definitely assigned to third grade and the former teacher of part of the subjects has given me good help. Of all the grades that is the one that I feel most able to cope with and having some of the very same books that we used in Calvert[66] will make it even easier. Of course, easy isn't quite the word for it for I will have 30 little squirmers of 18-20 nationalities and most of them spoiled army brats or Embassy offspring.

Letter: September 8, 1951

I am to be librarian! Will Tiddo please airmail me all she knows about running a library?!! But isn't it nice I won't have to teach? Osborne engineered that, bless him!! It means that I shall have study halls and maybe substitute when necessary, but I won't have lessons to prepare and papers to correct, so there will be more time for our bairns. And I'll have books around me, even if I don't have time to read. Things are in awful shape with the card files mixed up, many books lost, etc. I'm serious about help from Tiddo – any short texts on library technique would be appreciated for I want the library to be more than a storage place for books.

Letter: September 16, 1951

Osborne sent me over to the first-grade room to help test first grade applicants. They were such cute youngsters I would have loved to see almost all of them enter. Out of 45 first grade applicants we could take only 18 even though we are going to run two first grade sections. I told Dick that I would like to start a school for all those we couldn't take because many of them need our school more than many children we must take. Most of us feel that there is so much more that needs doing.

66. During the two years in Afghanistan Rebecca taught Wetherill and Os, and a few other students, using Calvert Correspondence School materials. This was her only previous teaching experience.

Letter: October 2, 1951

My hours have been changed slightly. Since I had no study hall first period I asked if I might not stay home that hour and keep the library open for reference and checking out books for a period after school closed.

School is really getting along very well and I was quite tickled to hear that two of Osborne's students have been making pleased remarks about his teaching. My study halls have had to take care of themselves for the last week or ten days for I have been busy recording the statistics on the physical exams that have been given. It gives me a chance to see all the student body and they are a nice bunch, on the whole.

The worst problem is my student assistant and he is a most efficient manager! He is rather older than others, bigger than any of the teachers and learns too easily for his own good. But he is a nice boy, if we can just guide him to use his abilities constructively.

Letter: October 15, 1951

Certainly you, Ret, are better equipped to do the guidance work that Dick is giving me. Today, in a few seconds, I will go over to one of Osborne's cheating problems. Won't have any privacy in the morning so hereafter she is to be asked to come in the afternoons and I'll try to find an opportunity to talk with her. Found a good book last night and have done a bit of prepping.

I am also to have a session with one of the problem teachers with whom Dick felt his talk made little impression. She has treated Os in a most unjust way[67] – I happened to witness one incident and was in a cold fury at the sadism she exhibited. The feeling about her runs thru all the grades she teaches. The other problem teacher, a Swiss man is elderly, blind in one eye and hard of hearing. Osborne sat in on one of his classes where he has trouble keeping order. The boys ganged up on Osborne later and asked him to come every day because they found it was interesting when they listened!! Osborne told them he had been interested, too, but he had other chores to do and they would have to be their own mentors.

67. I don't remember the Bible teacher, but do remember being skeptical of religious ceremonies and fanciful claims, and yet tolerant of the variety of ways people live. In chorus, I sang (quietly): "Onward Christian children, marching as to play!"

Letter: March 2, 1952

Os' problems won't be here next year – at least, Osborne told Dick that if they were we wouldn't be, for he thought that they were such a bad moral influence. It isn't only Os who has been suffering – in every class there is at least one victim – always boys. The Bible teacher has every one in a pet, especially the Buchers, who say that she has turned Joann so against the Bible that she doesn't even want to attend family worship! We object to her because she is such a liar. One of those spoiled people who must put herself in the right light at the expense of truth. Children notice that sort of thing mighty quickly.

Letter: October 21, 1951

My own work is shaping up a bit. The library is beginning to look like one – scads of books have been eliminated and the boy scouts have promised to paint my tables and chairs. The youngsters seem to enjoy coming and are really fine about being orderly even when I have to go out. Last year they used to have book battles in the library!

Tiddo's suggestions were a big help and gratifying since I found I was doing some things correctly! Library is for 5th to 11th grades with special libraries in 5th and 6th grade rooms.

As guidance counselor, skinned knees, headaches, lost articles and little brothers all come my way. Mothers, teachers and students bring their problems. It is interesting and varied and I have such a chance to know a large portion of the school.

Letter: November 12, 1951

I had to substitute one morning for the fourth-grade teacher and came home very sure that I was much happier in the library than teaching. That afternoon Dick came in for tea and told me he wanted me to work with some students on study habits – a chance remark made in a teachers' meeting got me into that. It means study for me but is a subject that I feel is most important.

Letter: December 4, 1951

Two girls from 10th have been suspended and spent the morning in the library before going home, weeping most of the time. The last hour I spent talking with them and one begged me to stay with them while they talked to Dick though I told her I couldn't help her, that it was her job to do. Don't I get into heart-pulling jobs?!

When the father of one girl was brought in his first remark was "What can I do to help?" If one had more parents as balanced and sincere... He blamed himself for not seeing more of his daughter so that he would have known what was going on before it became so serious. I admire that man.

Holiday Card, 1951

The Dutch Ambassador's daughter is in 4th grade where I have substituted quite often. They have taken to whooping whenever I appear, bless 'em. Rins said that I would speak quite sternly sometimes but she noticed there was a smile in my eyes at the same time. The Ambassador told her, "With such a sweet face she couldn't be unkind."!!! Maybe he shouldn't know me better!

Letter: February 13, 1952

Dick asked me to help with the recreation committee. Rick Pond, one of the young teachers on the committee, has been having trouble keeping control of his classes. He says that it is because he doesn't have time to prepare his lessons – though he is teaching only about half time already. Since I am at school twice as long as he, have four children, a husband and a house to care for, I told Dick that I felt I could not take on any more without it taking time from the children and I did not feel that was being fair to them. Since his own wife is strong on the point of having time for <u>her</u> children there wasn't much that he could say. He has found someone else.

Letter: August 16, 1952

Chuck Swan[68] is going to take over setting up the library. Though I had expected to be at school all morning Dick has scheduled me for only the first three periods in the morning. Osborne thinks he is a little self-conscious about Mary Ann's not teaching at all but I'm not arguing because there will still be parties to chaperone and I fear

68. A Community School teacher and special friend of the family. In about 1960 Wetherill and Os visited him in Washington DC where he worked.

I may be drafted for program planning which I dislike. Poor Osborne will have four hours of teaching, which, with his bookkeeping and management is going to be a terrific schedule.

Letter: October 19, 1952

Wednesday was a humdinger of a day. Os' violin teacher gave a concert at school at 2 o'clock. It was difficult because the piano cut up and made awful noises but Zorick was most good tempered about it and as usual gave an excellent performance. I brought him home for a cup of tea afterward and then we both had to run, he to a rehearsal and I to a parent-teachers meeting at school. We were all supposed to be in our rooms while the parents made a tour of the building and then we met in the auditorium and we teachers tried to assemble groups to chat about their questions before the meeting was opened for general discussion. It was in quite a fine spirit and only a few questions were ridiculous, including the European father who asked the principal to see that his little boy did not get so dirty at school!!!

It is a new departure for our students to have all their history, geography, social sciences and English courses lumped together, and much of it done as research without any textbook. They seem to like it and are getting to work with a fine display of energy and ingenuity. It makes more work for me since Pena doesn't know how to do research herself but it is such fun, I have a grand time every morning. The first week I spent the afternoons in the library, too, because Pena was scared and it looks as though I shall have to stick my head in quite often for she can't seem to keep order but I do hope that she will soon be able to manage by herself because my load at home is heavier this year. All three girls are taking piano lessons and Os needs some help with his violin (I play for him so that he can check his key) and all four usually have vocabularies, arithmetic tables or spelling words to listen to.

The library is such a joy to be in after the cramped, dark little hole we had last year. This year it is about 25 × 50 feet with lots of windows and a workroom for marking books. The gardener brings me fresh flowers three times a week and keeps some flowering potted plants in the windows so we look most attractive. Our enrollment is now up to 507 and there are still some more American children expected.

Scenes of Iranian Life

Overleaf: *Construction workers at Community School having lunch.*

A market street in Hamadan.

An enterprising individual provides shade on a Hamadan street.

Children playing in a doorway.

View across Tehran to the Alborz mountains.

View of Tehran, from a postcard bought in 1951.

The Post & Telegraph Building in Toopkhaneh Square, Tehran.

A Tehran neighborhood.

The Mausoleum of Imam Reza in Mashhad.

Brick bleachers at the Community School.

The new compound, with the front gate in the distance.

The carpenter, in typical striped pants, was making a set of swings for the school.

Workmen at lunch. In the sieve in front of them is a long piece of bread from which they tear off pieces.

Leveling the ground for a new lawn.

If you don't have a wheelbarrow, you make a substitute.

Two Community School gardeners. In the background, the head gardener goes over landscaping plans with Rebecca.

Gulam Hossain did everything related to the garden, including arranging flowers beautifully.

In Hamadan, Os riding as the oxen plod through the wheat.

A close-up of the threshing machine.

Bagging wheat in Hamadan.

Wetherill inspects the contents of a workman's bucket.

A water pumping system at Babolsar on the Caspian shore. If you don't have lumber, you make do.

Pulling water up with a rope. Note the traditional structures in the background.

A well on a street in Hamadan, with an elaborate structure to help pull up the water.

Two men peddle a machine to raise water in a well, with Wetherill and Os watching. Something off to the side has caught Rebecca's eye in the background.

Boys pumping water at the pensión that we stayed at in Babolsar on the Caspian.

A man shoulders his large burden, as Rebecca and Anne pass. They were on a hike near Tehran.

The load was balanced on a rope from his neck or shoulder and around the pole between his legs. It looks awkward but is effective.

Boys carrying water jugs in Hamadan.

Washing carpets at Cheshmeh Ali, near Tehran. The mineral waters strengthen the colors in the rugs.

A brick factory.

A pottery store in Hamadan.

On a street in Hamadan, sheep waiting for the butcher. Note the awning protecting the shop from the hot sun.

Melons for sale in Hamadan. The dome and minarets of a mosque are visible in the background.

An indoor bazaar in Hamadan.

Donkeys carrying wheat near Hamadan

A donkey train in Tehran.

Two men helping a loaded donkey cross a stream.

Chapter 23: Gardens

Letter: June 29, 1951

I know whereof the fame of Persian gardens has arisen though I have not yet seen a really super-duper one. In comparison to those we have known, these gardens are lovely and artistic[69]

We Went to School in Tehran

Never have I seen a house in Tehran or Shemiran without a garden. There is usually a *hoze* in the middle, a six-foot-deep pool to store water for sprinkling flowers. Around a *hoze* there is often a riot of color with brick or paved walks and a place to sit in the late afternoon or to sleep during the warm summer nights. A few trees will give shade but rarely will there be any grass unless the gardener has been trained by a European.

The *hoze* beside our house was a hazard to our household. One summer we discovered that the water level was too low for the ducks to get out of the pool. Shab was showing a green mold on his chest. It took the whole family and Batool to get the silly fellow out of the water. Demavand was quite willing to be rescued when we were wakened early one morning by his frightened yelping. I ran out onto the balcony in my nightgown to encourage the poor puppy who was clinging to the edge of the pool while Osborne tore downstairs with a trail of pajamaed children following pell-mell after him. They got the pup out of the water but he had skinned his legs badly and never again tried to drink from the *hoze*. Batool's little Mariam was just as anxious to get out of the water when she fell in, for she didn't know how to swim.

Letter: August 23, 1951

Now we have seen it – a typical fabulous Persian garden and how lovely it is. The entrance is very plain even to being rundown in appearance for the owner did not want the land confiscated by the former Shah. There is a large car park and a steep bank below. We went

69. Persian gardens were so famous so long ago that their name in Persian, *pairi-daeza*, was the source of our English word, "paradise."

down some steps and looked across a swimming pool set in a grove of trees. Two large tents gave space for eating and dressing. All around the pool were tuberous begonias in a great number of varieties and colors. At one side was an open space for games with brilliant zinnias against a shiny green hedge. We met several people who were there for a swim. Ruth Elder said that they were terribly upper crust but I don't remember just who they were – royal relatives of some kind.

We wound around and down some stone steps to a lower level with more flowers and a wading pool for children and then entered a long avenue going down to a second and larger pool. Water flows down the center of the avenue with rocks set in the *jube* (ditch) to make it ripple. The pool is at the bottom of a long series of terraces completely planted in flowers. It has several fountains and since water is scarce this summer the level was low enough for Wetherill to touch bottom all around. She can really swim with a good bit of splash and wasted effort but terrific enjoyment. She does a low dive fairly well but didn't try yesterday for the water was rather low.

Below the pool was the rose garden and I don't believe that I have ever seen any roses finer than those – huge, beautifully colored specimens and hundreds of them. The Prime Minister had gone there the day we had originally planned to go, and the Shah had been there two weeks ago more or less incognito. The hostess, a good friend of Community School, said that he and his party of twenty or twenty-five squealed like children and had a good time romping about though the French Minister tried to dive in a low spot and cracked open his scalp.

Diary: Notes; We Went to School in Tehran

Most gardeners object to having the flowers picked. I had a running feud with Mashtali all one summer. Quite often I literally ran to avoid an argument but I would pick flowers for the house. He tried to defeat me by picking flowers for me – the petals usually fell off in the process of handing them over, they were so old.

When he discovered that I continued picking fresh flowers he spied to discover when I came out for them and watered the garden just ahead of me. I switched from morning flower gathering to evening and then he thought he'd fix me. He kept the garden flooded for two weeks but he had to give in to save the plants from dying. I went right back as soon as the ground dried out.

When I gave some cuttings to friends he eyed them sourly and turned to glare as they passed. Looking up, he saw me grinning on the porch steps and greeted me with a curt and hopeless, "Salaam." The next spring he didn't say a word when he found me picking pansies the day after he had planted them. He just stared unhappily at me over the hedge.

Letter: April 4, 1952

Spring is really here, Mashtali has finally decided that he can't keep me from picking the pansies along our front walk and I have compromised by telling the children not to take the shortcut thru the hedge!

Picture Captions; We Went to School in Tehran

Eventually Mashtali decided that flower-picking was only one of my lesser peculiarities and we became sincere friends. He was a good friend even to the children. They taught him to say "Hello, jonnie" which means "Hello, darling" and he greeted them all that way.

Letter: June 8, 1952

We had a wild moment before Commencement began when Mrs. Carr found there were no flowers in the chapel. Mashtali and Ibrahim borrowed plants from Miss Chase's and Uncle Art's porches and things looked quite alright by the time the ambassador arrived. Mashtali scolded me for not telling him beforehand but his scolding is a friendly gesture nowadays. He is such a funny old nice man, I miss having him around. [This was after our move to the New Compound.] He came up to see us on his day off.

Chapter 24: Festivals

Letter: March 25, 1952; We Went to School in Tehran

March 21st is *No Ruz* which is New Year's Day in Iran and there are some pleasant customs.[70] As a holdover from Zoroastrian times, perhaps, there is a fire ceremony before the new year. Behind our house, Batool, our friend and servant, laid bundles of straw two feet apart in a series of three. When dark came the fires were lighted and Wetherill and Os and I went out to jump over the bonfires with Batool and her family. Once down and back is supposed to be enough but the children kept it up as long as the fire burned. Batool asked me to jump, too, so I went leaping over and much to my surprise neither fell into the fires nor singed my legs! It was quite appropriate for we hear that the significance is that one wishes that the yellow weakness or illness go out and the red strength of the fire enter in – Osborne [who was sick] watched from the window. Batool's elderly mother waited until the fires had died down to embers and then she picked up her skirts and hobbled across.

Letter: April 4, 1952

Yesterday we had another day of vacation – it was Thirteenth Day and quite a family holiday. [The 13th day after *No Ruz* marks the end of the holiday.] We understand that on that day most people go out into the country for a picnic, taking with them sprouted rice or beans which are broadcast. The unmarried girls say "to me a husband, in my husband's house, a baby in my arms," which strikes me as a pretty ambitious program for one year, if the girls are starting from scratch!

Letter: October 15, 1951; We Went to School in Tehran

Back in Tehran [from the Caspian] we hurried about the task of setting up school in the new building. It was *Muharram*, the month of mourning for the deaths of Mohammad's grandsons. Each night groups of boys and men attended mosques and paraded thru the streets. They carried banners and some had chains with which they beat themselves. As the climatic tenth day approached the tempo in-

70. In Iran, the year starts on the day of the spring equinox.

creased, there were more parades, men chanted longer and louder and rattled their chains more vigorously. It was like the *Penitentes* we remember in New Mexico, only these penitents lash themselves with chains and cut their heads with swords. We kept off the streets during the heat of the passion.

Living in a Muslim area with mosques in several directions, we heard the parades close to our walls far into the night. The last night there were candle parades representing the search for the body of Hussein.[71]

71. Hussein ibn Ali was Muhammad's grandson, killed in 680 CE along with many members of his family. This, as well as the earlier killing of his father, Ali, began the conflict between Shiite and Sunni Moslems.

Chapter 25: Zoroastrians

Letter: February 17, 1953; We Went to School in Tehran

Our Zoroastrian friend, Rustam Shahzadi, came to dinner and what a fine time we had talking with him of his faith. He is a teacher and must be a good one for our questions were well and fully answered. "You Christians have love and kindness as your central theme. We have Truth," he told us. For that reason education is thought to be of primary importance. Girls have been educated and women have been given a voice in the religious and community life of Zoroastrians even under the early Muslim rule of Iran, when other women remained secluded and often illiterate.

Our children were pleased with a little situation that arose when we sat down to dinner. Mr. Shahzadi asked if we did not say a blessing. Osborne explained our quiet thanksgiving and asked if the Zoroastrians said a prayer. We were told that they do and asked if he would say one. He explained that he would give thanks for fire, water, air, food, and all good things and then, in a melodious singsong, he recited a prayer in the ancient Avestan language of the Zoroastrians. Today only the priests understand the scriptural tongue but they always translate each part of their services and prayers so that the people may know what is being said.[72]

Last Sunday we went to visit the Zoroastrian temple – an old building whose rugs and furnishings were quite shabby. In the center of the building is an enclosed place with a window in one side so we could look inside and see the huge urn in which the eternal fire burns. The air was pleasantly scented with sandalwood and there was peace and quiet in the atmosphere. Behind is a hall where funeral services are conducted. People do not go to the home to mourn with the bereaved family but come to this hall at specified times to pray and eulogize.

We went into the Zoroastrian boys high school which is quite

72. "Rustam Shahzadi, a trained priest, but not a daily practicing one, was a leader of the Tehran [Zoroastrian] community. Trained in Bombay, he was acknowledged as the most scholarly of the Iranian priests." (*Mute Dreams, Blind Owls, and Dispersed Knowledges: Persian Poesis in the Transnational Circuity,* by Michael M. J. Fischer, Durham, NC: Duke University Press, 2004, p. 397)

an old building but neatly painted. There were some furious games of ping pong going on, a volley ball game and some basketball practice. Classes were let out just then so we did not see them in academic action. I noticed that some of the boys took a shortcut thru an open window to get out to the playground as quickly as possible so I judge that they are much the same as all other boys!

We were tremendously impressed by the kindergarten where all the children were fresh and washed, in clean white coveralls and pinafores with rooms of soft and varied coloring and more interest and initiative than you usually see in local schools. A quick visit to the girls' high school was not long enough to see all the large building where 800 girls study. We popped into an English class where there were 45 students and the teacher told me that she was sorry that there was not enough chance for the girls to practice the language. The girls giggled and a few brave souls replied when I called goodbye as we left.

Chapter 26: Women

Diary: Notes

The chador moves with a graceful sweep and swish, but seems a nuisance. It is held in the mouth, even though not always clean. The black veil can be refined with a variety of small, gay, flowered patterns. Many women cling to the chador.

Chadorred women of the lower class have their arms covered to the wrist and hair hidden – sometimes only one eye shows. One such girl shed her reserve briefly. My friend, Mim [Zoradnick], asked her *bajeh* [house cleaner] if she wouldn't like to swim (or splash since of course she had never had a chance to swim) in their swimming pool in the garden. She explained that the girl must bathe, soap well all over and rinse before getting in. One day she looked out to find the girl beside the pool with a bucket of water soaping her bareness thoroughly. When well-scrubbed she popped into the pool and what a glorious time she had splashing around, jumping out, running, skipping and leaping in joyful and exaggerated imitation of the water sporting she had watched. Mim hoped the neighbors weren't looking. When the *bajeh* left the compound she was as demure as ever in her chador!

We Went to School in Tehran

Because so many refugees have come to Tehran, the city is more cosmopolitan than other cities of the country. Even in Tehran, however, one sees the picturesque along with the mundane. Women with sleeves to their wrists and flowing ankle length semi-circular veils walk the streets beside bareheaded women in sleeveless dresses.

Once in a while, under the veil you notice the straight black pants, short pleated skirt and gay overblouse of a village woman. I heard an intriguing story of this particular costume which was once worn all over Iran. It seems there was an earlier Shah who spent quite a bit of time in Paris and particularly enjoyed the ballet. When he came back to Iran he missed the whirling pleated skirts of the dancers and decreed that all Iranian women should wear full, abbreviated skirts. The straight blouse and black pants were a concession to Persian modesty and created a most attractive costume, which is worn by many women still.

We Went to School in Tehran

Some of our friends in Tehran told us that a weekly visit to the bathhouse is essential to keeping clean, even though one bathes at home. I suspect that the motivation is as much social as hygienic. Women carry elaborate equipment to the baths. Aside from towel and washcloth, a comb, and soap in a crocheted bag, there's a big rug or quilt carryall, a fancy cloth on which to spread articles, a metal tray on which to stand while drying, a pitcher, a triangle of cloth with which to tie up the hair after shampooing, and a pleated "modesty skirt," an 18-inch strip worn as an apron so that the body is never completely exposed. A piece of pumice is used for scrubbing elbows and feet, and a softer, more porous stone rubs the rest of the body clean.

We Went to School in Tehran

Iranian women commonly touch up their hair with dye. As they age they use red dye instead of black to conceal the white strands. Thus the mixture of red and black hair reddens with the passage of time until, like Batool's mother, nothing but gaily hennaed hair is left.

Diary: Notes

In church, two women I knew stood to sing. A man helpfully found the place and held the hymnal so they could see the Persian script – but one could read only Armenian and the other not at all.

Diary: Notes

Dr. Sabra Hanumi told me of a woman who runs a business: she was the first person to bring auto taxies to Tehran.

Letter: February 4, 1955

A few women now appear at demonstrations and once I saw a woman in a truck speaking to a crowd. In a land where women have always been kept under a veil, this may be very good political maneuvering on the part of the Communists.

Letter: March 25, 1952; We Went to School in Tehran

During the New Year holiday I wanted to take Osborne, who had been seriously ill [with malaria], to a friend at the American Hospital in Tabriz. It was necessary to get a special permit to visit any towns at a distance from Tehran, especially those near the borders. We wanted Osborne to stay in Tabriz for treatment while the children and I returned to Tehran for school.

After a lot of trouble getting separate passports and making separate applications, when I went down to pick up the permit I found that they had issued only one for all four of us. That meant we would have to stick together. I blew up emphatically, waved my arms around and sputtered what Farsi I knew. The clerk drew himself up to his full, more than six-foot height and glared down at me.

"The police department thinks that you should stay in Tabriz with your husband until he is well," he informed me!!!!

Speech to Federated Women: February 19, 1955

I would credit several things for the difference in the attitude of Iran and Afghanistan to their women. Iran's borders have always been open to foreigners, whereas Afghanistan was closed until about 20 years ago – you didn't go in unless you were invited and few people were. There have been Armenians and Nestorian Christians for centuries in Iran, and Zoroastrians who educated their girls secretly when they were not supposed to years ago. Zoroastrian women have always been taken in as part of the religious faith and shared worship with their men. Muslim women in Iran still have to go to a side room or aisle, which is carefully secluded from the men and they have no real religious education. They get what they can from the men and old wives tales – you can imagine how diluted their knowledge of their religion can be.

There are schools for girls all over Iran, even in villages where people are most conservative. The father of the present Shah emancipated women and forbade the use of the rather pretty veil Iranian women wore. That law is now in abeyance and many women wear the veil. These can be quite pretty and inexpensive and they cover up what is underneath. A woman can be the epitome of fashion in a black silk chador[73] and wear any old rag under it. If she is careful, no one will know.

Batool used to wear a chador when we lived in a compound where the other women were Muslims. When we moved to a compound where the other women were Armenians and had never been veiled, Batool stopped wearing the chador. I noticed that quite often women who would usually wear a chador, would take it off and wear a bandana if they went out with a foreign woman. Batool's sister, a Muslim, went shopping with me in the Old Bazaar where the most conservative policies held. I was quite surprised that she boldly went bareheaded as I did.

I had a solid argument with the mission when our Yeksabet's son, Sako, was to be married and wanted to continue to live in the compound. Married children were supposed to move out on their own, but when I mentioned that Yeksabet had no other man to depend upon, her son was allowed to stay. Life can be very hard in Iran for a woman who doesn't have a man to depend upon.

73. A shawl worn over the head and shoulders, it can be pulled across the face for more privacy.

Chapter 27: Politics

[In the 1950s in Iran a mighty contest was going on between monarchists and populists. Other powerful interests were the religious traditionalists (the mullahs), and the merchant class (the bazaar). This was the latest turn of the wheel as ancient Persia struggled to become modern Iran.]

Letter: July 16, 1951

People have been uniformly pleasant; business and pleasure has gone on as usual except for a weekly demonstration in some square. This morning Osborne got up at 5:30 to play tennis and everything is quiet. Taxies are now beginning to pass the compound gate, I hear an early huckster calling *aloo-baloo* (cherries).

[The Majlis (Parliament) passed legislation on March 17, 1951, three months before we arrived, reclaiming Iranian oil from a British company (now part of BP) that had been granted a monopoly in 1933.]

We Went to School in Tehran

Gas pumps were being repainted the day we arrived in Tehran. The name of the Anglo-Iranian Oil company was being effaced because the nationalization of Iranian oil had taken place – conferences were still being held behind the elaborate iron grill of the Parliament gate. The man in the street talked a good bit about oil but most of the time was little effected by the tremendous course of events.

It was uncomfortable for us that near our back door was Peace House, a Communist youth club and propaganda center. It was twice raided by the police when we would hear shooting and shouting. One day Os successfully ducked a ricocheting bullet that zinged over his head as he scampered home thru the garden.

"The next time, I'm going to fall down flat," he reported. Fortunately there was no next time.

Crowds gathered around the gate to the Parliament building or at the University sometimes, and there were occasional riots but these were quite remarkably localized. It was interesting to us that these disturbances usually kept to fairly regular hours, stopping at noon for lunch and siesta, beginning again about four or five o'clock. By nightfall, almost invariably, the streets were deserted once more. Sometimes we would see store-front shutters half lowered as merchants kept business going while scanning the street for trouble

One of our friends told us of watching from a balcony during a demonstration. There was a large meeting being held at the Parliament several blocks away. Gradually, just beneath the balcony a crowd gathered. A man mounted a box and began to harangue in an excited tone. He damned the Americans and other foreigners. He was making good headway when a young man on a bicycle came pedaling furiously down the street. In a scant moment the speaker, the crowd and even the box had vanished. It was done so smoothly and quietly that the break-up was scarcely noticeable. Just young people by twos and threes strolling in all directions and melting into doorways. Scarcely had they broken up when an army truck rumbled down the street hunting just such groups as had met under the balcony.

Standing last night on the balcony, overlooking the little church, with quiet towering sycamores and moonlight shining on our sleeping children, it was hard to believe that there had been strife in our city. From our compound we had heard some distant shouting and what sounded like fire crackers. We knew there was to be a rally for they are always announced and we try to avoid that street or square at the time of the meeting.

Letter: July 16, 1951

Bob and Carol Bucher had invited everyone to their house for a hymn sing. Osborne and I planned to go as soon as the children were settled in bed but from our balcony we could still hear sporadic rifle fire and decided not to go even as far away as the Buchers, although it is only on the other side of the school building. Our conversation was in French so that the children were unaware that we suspected the rally had gotten a little out of hand.

Before Wetherill and Os were asleep the telephone rang and Osborne went down, not knowing who was still at home. Ruth and John Elder were both there and talked to a friend who said that a group of communists had made a big noise, the nationalists had tried to shut them up, a hand grenade was tossed and trouble started. The rumor is that quite a few lives were lost but the difficulty was entirely localized – or at least there were no roving bands around our streets. The only shots we heard were in just one area. This is the only evidence that we have had of unrest.

Of course we realize that something might go out of control but it doesn't seem as alarming from here as it is presented to you in the U.S. where there are strikes and riots and bloodshed, too, sometimes. It is not that we are unaware of the tension but somehow we have faith that such outbreaks as last night will be controlled and localized. Osborne and I have a bit of nagging worry, that the children not be involved in unpleasantness but there is no indication now that they will be and we see no reason why we should not do the job we have to do.

Letter: April 4, 1952

Is the press being hysterical again? We are not in the least and life goes on as usual. There was a day or two when the more prudent stayed at home, but there are times in USA when you avoid certain areas for a time. There seemed to be a perfect control of the situation here, which is all important. So – don't worry about us.

[Rebecca didn't write about politics very often because was more interested in people themselves. However, another reason she stayed away from the topic in her letters, is shown in the following note that was hand carried to Ret by a friend.]

Letter: June 18, 1952

There seems something so much more intimate about a letter that is to be delivered by hand. We are enclosing a pair of enameled earrings which aren't much, but light for Addie to carry.

I don't usually talk politics because of censorship (probably why letters come opened). As we see it from here the government is in a ticklish position. Practically bankrupt, in disfavor at home and abroad and terribly pushed by Communist propaganda. There is a very strong

Communist party which has been more or less driven underground for the last few months. We haven't had any *shalook*, as disturbance is called, for quite a while. Most difficulties have been pretty well localized and surprisingly quickly brought under control. The police seem to do well and if they continue to get paid will probably do all right. We don't feel in personal danger though we realize the potential danger of a blow-up is greater than in the U.S. At the moment Mission – Gov't relations seem to be improving.

[Mohammad Mosaddeq was a populist who opposed the Shah. He had a long history as a leader in the Iranian *Majlis* and he became Prime Minister a month after the oil was nationalized in 1951. Many factions fought over how to govern Iran; they were conservative and liberal, religious and secular, monarchist and democratic. Finally, the Shah forced Mosaddeq to resign.]

Diary: Notes

Mosaddeq is out as Prime Minister. Tanks were drawn up before the *Majlis*, soldiers and truckloads of reserves all along Naderi. Our taxi drove to Saadi Circle. There soldiers were drawn up at the end of the street so we had to turn around and go back to a *kucheh* that took us across farther up. Typical unfamiliarity with traffic control: they didn't block the street at a turn-off place. One policeman was there but nobody paid any attention to him.

The Armenian minority is fearful. Stones were thrown during a funeral procession thru the poor part of the city to a cemetery.

On the way to church the next day, we saw crowds gathering. The Old Bazaar and most shops were closed, few women were on the streets, men were on balconies and at windows overlooking *Majlis* square. Part of Naderi was cut off and so our taxi turned south but a little way down the street the cars ahead began to turn around in a hurry. The crowd began running toward us with scared, tense faces. A truckload of police farther down spilled out and with flaying blackjacks dove into the melee. Our driver turned quickly into a *kucheh* [an alley] with running men and got thru into a quiet street.

[After three days of rioting the Shah had to reappoint Mosaddeq as Prime Minister. The contest continued.]

Diary: February 28 – March 4, 1953

On Saturday, February 28th, 1953, Ruhie was here to help with the cleaning. About 3 o'clock Yadallah called to tell her to go home immediately, that the Shah had abdicated and a big *shalook* was boiling up. [The news was premature and the Shah remained for the time being.] I went over to school and found that they had known for two hours that there was an emergency. Yeksabet was excited and had gone to see if John Elder would take Ruhie home. John was so wonderfully calm about it. "Yes, she may go with me but I have one or two hours work to do first," was his reply. Almost 30 years in this country has given him some perspective on *shalooks.*

Rumors were rife of course. Haikin got a paper at 3 o'clock saying the Shah had abdicated, that the country was under control of four people including Mosaddeq and Gulam Reza, the Shah's brother, who is considered rather a political rascal by some. The Shah was to leave the country at four o'clock. Osborne's first reaction was that this was planned well ahead in order to have the papers on the street so soon. Later we heard a rumor that the crisis was because Mosaddeq wanted cut all revenues being sent to the Queen Mother and Princesses whom Mosaddeq had insisted must leave the country. The Shah was adamant but offered to compromise, cut their allowances and spend the rest on the students who are abroad and have been short of funds due to the economic crisis. There were probably more basic reasons than that.

A large group gathered around the palace protecting the departure of the Shah, and another group at Mosaddeq's house stormed his gate with a jeep. Three were killed, we heard. Mosaddeq is reported to have climbed down a ladder in his red p.j.s and escaped over a wall to one of his neighboring houses which he had rented to Point Four. An 11 o'clock curfew was declared so that Osborne and I had only one square dance after Wetherill's party. Some of her guests stayed home because of the difficulties.

Sunday things were quite calm though when we came home from church we noticed that more stores than usual had their iron shutters pulled down. Police made only a single line of traffic approach the *Majlis*.[74] There were small boys and men climbing all over the *Majlis* gate and a truck drawn up in front had a mullah exhorting the crowd. Tanks and truck loads of soldiers were around and there was a tenseness and restlessness in the crowds, but good order.

On Monday, school had few students and many left at noon when a rumor raged that Mosaddeq had resigned. There were reports of crowds, shooting and knifing, but in our compound there were no reverberations, near as we were to the *Majlis*. We did not go out though others did. Yeksabet said it was hard to find food because most of the shops were closed.

Tuesday there were fewer students in school and more left at noon when word got around that the *Tudehs*[75] were going to have a meeting at the *Majlis* gate. The rumor today is that Mosaddeq is making a pact with Kashani[76] and the *Tudehs* – strange bedfellows. We heard that the Baktiari tribes were coming to town to protect the queen whose father was Baktiari (and mother German).

Newspapers began explaining that the Shah had expected to leave for reasons of "health." We saw in the French paper later that the Queen would go alone. Wonder if they are busting up – no heir in three years. It is rather late for an heir to pull the country together.

People walked down the street as though strolling. I heard that flying squads of *Tudehs* were out demanding death to the Shah. My feeling is that many in the country as a whole want the Shah, for that reason the Communists feel they must get rid of him.

On Wednesday we went to a reception for Herrick Young, head of the International House Association, and were told there that Stalin had died but it was not until Saturday that we heard it really occurred. Rumors were just as unreliable about that as about the local situations. It meant that the *Tudehs* let up on their activities to mourn which was all to the good.

74. The *Majlis* is the Iranian parliament.
75. The Tudeh Party was (and is) an Iranian communist party.
76. Abol-Ghasem Kashani was a nationalist and a leader of the Majlis.

Probably you have been hearing as accurate information as you did about the earthquake.[77] We had school every day and though there were tense moments we neither heard nor saw much of the activity. Rumors ran riot so that we believed nothing and simply waited, avoiding the streets for a few days.

We Went to School in Tehran

One soon learns to feel the vast expanse of the history and culture of Iran so that present day events become just another step on a long trek. For a study group I was asked to prepare Iranian historical dates "from the beginning." The Assyrian King Shalmaneser II who conquered Media, the northern part of Iran, in 836 BC seemed like a beginning to me. The lecturer glanced at my list of dates and suggested that we start a little further back.

"About 2,000 BC,..." he began. With a jerk I realized how ancient the history of this country really is.

When viewed from the perspective of history, the recent events of conflicting influences in Iran have some of the monotony of repetition. There has been a continual wash of different cultures across the Iranian plateau: Arab, Mongol, Armenian, Turk, Russian, English, German, French – even the American imprint is felt for many of the taxi drivers speak American slang because they drove cars for American soldiers who were in Iran during World War II, or they studied in American Mission schools.

[The confrontation we had witnessed reached a climax two months after we left Iran. Mosaddeq forced the Shah to abdicate and a U. S. backed coup brought him back. He reigned another quarter century until the conservative religious government now leading Iran came to power in 1979.

Many years later Rebecca told us that the whole time we lived

77. Rebecca meant the reports they were reading in the U.S. about the political situation were probably as inaccurate as what they read about the earthquake three weeks before which was almost unnoticeable in Tehran, despite press reports.

in Tehran she kept a packed suitcase under the bed, prepared for a quick departure. We children didn't know this. We were simply busy being children.]

Travels

Overleaf: Taxi in Hamadan with Os, Rebecca, and Wetherill squeezed in. Osborne took the picture.

Once a year the seniors had a free day to take a trip. This time they planned a picnic by a river in Galandawak. Rebecca, Osborne and Os went along. In the first picture Rebecca is seen climbing into the back of a truck, the sort of challenge she enjoyed. After a ride in the countryside there was a long walk to a river where hotdogs were roasted. It was a long and very pleasant day.

We planned a two week vacation in the Presbyterian Mission guest house in Hamadan. A taxi picked us up in front of our house in the New Compound.

Typical buses encountered along the way.

There stops at shaded tea houses. At the table are Rebecca, Wetherill, Yeksabet and Os.

The guest house, called Nur Mahal.

A pond for swimming.

Wetherill and Os exploring the gardens.

A set of memorial inscriptions, called Ganj Nameh, are cared on a mountain beside what was an important trade route. They praise Darius and Xerxes who ruled the Persian Empire 2500 years ago. They are in three languages: Persian, Babylonian and Elamite.

A waterfall near Ganj Nameh.

Wetherill, Os and Rebecca on the ruins of Ecbatana, the summer residence of the kings of the Medes. Hamadan is below, with Mount Alvand in the distance.

Outside of Tehran, droshkies were commonly used as taxies.

The tomb of Esther and Mordacai in Hamadan.

The entrance to the tomb, built very low to force visitors into a reverent posture.

The Lion of Hamadan, carved on orders of Alexander in memory of his friend, Hephaestion, in 324BCE. Our guide is remonstrating with the boys who were carving their initials in the monument.

Os watching a friend, Montazami, as he paints the scene.

Osborne and Os climbed the mountain, Yakchal. The name means ice pit, and in August there was still snow at the top. Our group were Park Johnson and his son, Peter. It was a thrilling and exhausting day, Osborne reacting to the former and Rebecca to the latter.

The Chalus Road, from Tehran to the Caspian Sea, is a remarkable engineering feat and very beautiful.

In a traditional village near the Caspian, a young man runs to get in the picture with Wetherill.

Wetherill investigates an ingenious irrigation system. The low domes of a mosque are behind her.

Canopied row boats ferry people on the river and out to the beaches.

Wetherill insisted on helping row.

A fishing boat comes in from the sea.

This boat brought ice to the Caspian fisheries.

On the Caspian beach, Wetherill talking with a visitor and the manager of a nearby hotel.

We made friends with a honeymoon couple staying in our pensión.

The mausoleum of Reza Shah, the father of the last Shah of Iran. It was destroyed in 1980 during the Iranian Revolution.

Ruins near Tehran.

Wetherill admires the carved stone mural at a pool where carpets were washed in the mineral water. It was made in about 1818 for Fath Ali Shah who liked to come to bathe.

The whole family joined a group hiking in the Alborz mountains. You will find Rebecca, Osborne, Wetherill, Os, Margie and Anne in these pictures.

Chapter 28: Shemiran

Letter: December 4, 1951

Saturday was a lovely fall day and weren't we surprised when three Irvines, four Buchers and one guest, and six Cressons (if we may all be called such) all arrived at the main gate at exactly the specified hour – 8:30 AM!!! We carried our lunches and looked surprisingly jaunty for people whose old clothes are really old. We meandered down the *kucheh* to a bus stop. Several buses were too full to take us all and since we were off on a hike together we didn't separate. Finally, we rode up the avenue named for the Shah toward the snow tipped mountains. At Shemiran we changed buses and rode on closer to the mountains. Shemiran is the summer suburb, eight or ten miles from town and directly under the towering bare mountains that shield us from the north.

At the end of the bus line we started our hike. The little village there lay beside a stream. Instead of going thru the village we turned to cross the brook. There was a mill grinding wheat which we inspected, scarcely able to see the big stone that was turned by water power for it was in a dark little room. Our path led along the stream all the way, first on one side, then on the other, passed garden patches, and up into the close, crowded canyon that climbed to *Haft Hoze* which means Seven Pools. Above the pools we found a sunny bend of the stream with a nice place to park ourselves – until it proved to be the middle of the path followed by donkeys and coolies bringing fuel down from the hills, which kept us from becoming rooted to the spot. How they found the fuel, I don't know for the hills are all as bare as can be.

It had been cold until we got to walking, then Mary Ann began to shed – a coat, a sweater, a scarf, mittens, a lumber shirt but she still had on long woolen underwear belonging to Dick, woolies of her own, corduroy slacks, a polo shirt and two pairs of sox! The sun was hidden behind the hills. All the children enjoyed scrambling around the rocks – we had use for the First Aid kit we always carry – and I turned the heel of my current sock. A bus was waiting for us when we got back to the village and we found that we were ready to sit down for tea when we got home.

One time we made the mistake of delaying until nine o'clock on a Friday evening when we had been picnicking in Shemiran. Crowds of other people had done the same and were waiting to board the buses. We joined the mass. When a bus arrived there was a great push and it wasn't gentle. We failed to get on during three attempts.

"This time you push too," Osborne told Os and me, when the fourth bus arrived. Having his arms full with an unwieldy lunch box Osborne prodded Os forward with his knee.

"Let's get out," Os wailed trying to drag me aside, but I was held firmly to the ground. One man was standing on the heel of my *giveh* and another had his foot planted on my toe. The bus assistant noticed our difficulty and kindly hoisted Os aboard while he pushed the man on my toe aside so that I could clamber on. The helper put his arm behind me to keep people from pushing me up the steps on my face. Osborne yanked a man aside and was the last man on. Men on the rear seat squeezed together so that I could sit down, two boys made room for Os, and Osborne sat on the lunch box all the way to Tehran.

Chapter 29: Ditch Day

Letter: May 27, 1953

Thursday was Ditch Day when all the seniors ditched classes and went on a picnic. They asked Chuck Swan, Osborne and me to chaperone and included Os in the invitation. Osborne said at first that Os had to stay in class but it happened that the two O's had planned to do some climbing today and tomorrow but Osborne felt that he had too much work to take so much time. We decided that one day out of school for fun – in six years of faithful attendance – wouldn't do too much harm. It pleased Os no end and the seniors found him a pleasant companion.

We assembled in front of school with all the high school classes looking out of their windows in dejection. We rode in a truck – standing up because it was so bumpy. It was a pleasant ride up to a valley we had not seen before. It is called Galandawak and is beautifully green with bare mounds of mountains all around. We passed some nomad camps and one camel train on the road. There were fifty-six camels which is rather large for a nomad group. One camel disliked the sound of the truck and scrambled up a high bank much to the distress of the little boy who was tied on top of the load. The people seemed friendly and smiled when we waved.

We tramped across country to a spot the youngsters knew beside a river. There was grass and some trees, rocks for sunning and sheep which smelled! Three of the boys started a charcoal fire in a shallow pit while the rest of us played softball on a bumpy field. I was scorekeeper with a heap of stones to keep me straight. Osborne hit multiple base hits until he was winded and then was umpire.

As soon as the fire was ready, we were eager to eat. I grinned to myself – seeing these children of many nations and creeds roasting their hot dogs. When the driver asked if there were pork in the hotdogs one of the Jewish boys evaded and told him to *befarmite* which is a general phrase meaning to enter, sit down, eat or take some. Mooshie Namordi[78] told me that it wouldn't hurt him if he didn't know what

78. Mooshie was one of Osborne's students and our friend. His family were Iraqi Jews who had to leave that country. We kept in close touch after he moved to the U.S.

was in it! We sat on rocks in a circle around the campfire and Chuck read some amusing poems and stories after lunch, then some slept and the rest walked. I volunteered to watch camp but had several companions, either sleeping or reading, and a shepherd and several little boys. I suspect that the latter would have rifled the knapsacks if no one were there. I was pleased that everyone picked up the camp and doused the fire before we left. It was interesting to hear the very American songs that the youngsters sang – and how well they knew them.

It was a very enjoyable day though we all came home with sunburned noses and rather tired. Later Osborne said that in the whole twelfth grade there isn't a single lemon. They are all nice youngsters. Quite an exceptional class!

where he had a successful career as an engineer with Texas Instruments in the early days of computers. It was heartwarming to see Mooshie at Rebecca's memorial service in Mount Holly, NJ in 1998.

Chapter 30: Mamazon

Letter: March 7, 1953

We had a most enjoyable day, yesterday, when we all went to Mamazon, one of the Near East Foundation villages. The Zoradnicks were laying the foundation for their house which is to be the first staff house built in the village. The Hitemans took us out after Quaker Meeting. Bud and Alice have two terrors of children six and seven, but they are awfully nice people from near Utica, New York. They have a dairy farm and decided they wanted to do something constructive for somebody else so they came out to Iran for two years. The family is adjusting very well and making a good contribution to their project.

We saw the poultry project where they have model houses, incubators and such. They are trying to raise the standard of the village poultry by exchanges – a village chicken for a Foundation one, village eggs for Foundation eggs – and I realized that I had forgotten that chickens and eggs could grow so big! John showed us his mechanical set-up, the garage, water and electric plant. The village wants to have electricity and are planning a consumers' co-op which will sell electricity, among other things.

We walked around the village. Saw their pure water spigots at corners, the women washing their vegetables and dishes and a cute little girl, only about three years old, scouring the cooking pot with dirt. A tinsmith was covering bowls and pots with tin because copper is not good to cook in unless it is plated. We were intrigued to see the bellows set up in an ingenious way. A tunnel is dug at an angle from the surface to a hole about 8 inches in diameter and a foot-and-a-half from the entrance to the tunnel. A double-lunged goatskin bag is operated to force air thru the tunnel into the hole where a charcoal fire is built. In that way, the fire can be controlled and a high heat blown up when required.

The houses have domed tops and there are usually three rooms for living, cooking and storing, but there are no windows. We looked over one low wall to find a neat yard with a tiny fenced chicken yard and a woman weaving a rug. It was a crude runner, not made like the carpets, but on a twenty-inch loom stretched along the ground. The woman straddled the loom as she wove.

We came home at sunset and had fun singing in spite of the dust that went down our throats. Today most of us have pink noses from being in the sun more than usual.

Chapter 31: Hamadan

[Hamadan is the ancient city of Ecbatana. It is on the banks of a river that runs through a broad plain suitable for agriculture, with hills that can aid in defense. At an altitude of 5900 feet, it has been the summer destination of kings and of missionaries. It was a capital of the Medes, and then the Achaemenids (who were overthrown by Alexander), and later the Parthians. The Greek historian Herodotus, 2500 years ago, wrote that Ecbatana was as big as Athens and had seven concentric walls, the innermost ones made of silver and gold.]

Letter: August 16, 1952

Ret, now that we have heard that you are doing so well [after an operation for breast cancer] we are going to go to Hamadan for two weeks. The Buchers will come down on Wednesday with an Iranian boy so there will be eight of us at Nur Mahal – a garden just outside of Hamadan. We are going to splurge and go by car for I haven't been able to get my usual pep back. In two weeks we will come back and try to get a permit to go to the Caspian for a few days. By then school will be ready to open.

Letters: August 20 and September 28, 1952;
Diary: August 18-30, 1952; We Went to School in Tehran

We left Tehran, Monday at 8:30 AM, in a blue "Studebake – air," the driver with a pleasant grin wrinkled face. He pointed out melons, grapes and squash that grew in fields along the way and helped to buy a watermelon at Qazvin. Mosaddeq's villages were in the distance south of our road. In Aveh he found a table for us under matting of a row of *chai-hawnas* along the street. Buses stopped with passengers. Many Arabs on pilgrimage – men with their square head cloths and corded anchors, women with flowing black burqas and a black head shawl. Many of them wore a thin black veiling completely covering their faces. The men mounted a platform six feet above the lunch tables to face Mecca and say their noon prayers.

Later, crossing a wide desert, I was surprised to see patches of wheat growing among the thorny tufts of camel grass. The road rose easily among the many folds of the Khargan mountain range until we came out onto the Hamadan plain. The main streets of the town stretched wide and straight toward a circle in the center. Single story shops, many horse drawn carriages and donkeys gave a rural aspect quite different from Tehran.

We came to Nur Mahal and were met by a great assortment of people including Yeksabet, who came to cook assisted by a village woman, and Rahman, the gardener, and his wife, a peasant woman who spoke Turkish and wore black straight legged pants under her dress and a white shawl over her head. She stood around gawping while we unpacked, with a daughter peeking over her shoulder.

Nur Mahal is a "garden" – not one of the formal Persian gardens but a little farm with a house that is mostly porch. The house is a two-story affair with dining, servant and kitchen quarters downstairs and upstairs a wide passageway in the middle with dressing rooms on each side. A screened porch goes all the way around and beds are set up where needed. By the time our contingent reached 17 we had beds all the way around and just one small sitting area with too few chairs though most of us sat on the floor. Needless to say there was little privacy but such nice people that we thoroughly enjoyed ourselves.

It smells like Virginia with new mown hay all around the house and looks like New Mexico with the green valley below bare craggy mountains in the south – north we have a view far across a plain to the brown adobe town of Hamadan. It is at an elevation of about 6,000 ft. and cool enough for a blanket at night.

The next morning Osborne and the children walked to town. In the afternoon Jamileh came to stay with us. She is a little girl whom Leree Chase had taken in to educate. Leree is now in the U.S. and Jamileh was going to go to school here in Hamadan but the hospital is being closed due partly to shortage of staff and there won't be a home for Jamileh. She will stay here until we or the Buchers return to Tehran, then she will probably go to the English run school in Isfahan.

Wednesday Osborne and three children walked south toward the mountains – across fields for two hours, up from the road, across people's porches, along a path to the next porch above. Everyone was very pleasant. Coming down thru a garden they found themselves on top of a farmer's mud roof where it sprang from the hillside. They called down to the farmer to inquire how to descend from his roof. The Buchers and Montezami, a young painter, arrived in time for tea.

Settled in with our larger family, wrote letters and awaited the Park Johnsons [from Beirut]. Fifteen of us are here now. On the ground around the house each morning we find broken bits of sky – or so the blue gentians look. Oxen are treading out the wheat. The children ride the creaking wooden paddle wheel that breaks the heads off, ready for winnowing.

Friday evening Cody Allen, Burt and Betty Dyson and three children came to picnic supper on the point overlooking town. Hamburgers, cukes, tomatoes, coffee, raw carrots, grapes and *sangak*. That is a long piece of bread that gets its name from being baked on stones (*sang* is stone). Sometimes you get the stones along with the bread.

The next day our families went climbing up 11,000 feet Yakhchal (Icebox) which is one of the highest peaks of the Alvand range. There is a snow pocket which lasts all summer and gives the mountain its name. Joy was the only female to attempt it. The rest of us had a cozy lazy day with our reading and embroidery and often mentioned how much more comfortable we were than the climbers. They began drifting in, Bob, Joy and Montazemi who had not gone all the way to the top at 7:15 PM. The four Johnsons at 7:45 and Osborne and Os at 8:15. The trail was not difficult but it was a long way and my men in not too good condition. They were cheerful but obviously tired and I was furious at such useless expenditure of energy.[79]

Ellen Nicholson came in to meet Cuyler Young for a short visit – it brought our family to 17 when Cuyler arrived at the end of supper.

Sunday the Johnsons left after breakfast and Cuyler after lunch. Jamileh's brother came for her so our family seemed quite small at nine. Carol gasped at one point, "Isn't this a restful vacation?" It seemed more like a rat race then.

I am doing a great deal of resting (reading at the same time).

79. Rebecca worried when we did not return until after dark, and I was very tired: my legs were shaking with fatigue. However, she missed our elation on summiting the mountain and the comfortable time we had together on the long walk home. One of Osborne's passions in his youth had been mountain climbing. I remember noticing how quickly he disappeared when Rebecca's anger became apparent.

Osborne is going to do a few hours preparation for his math and physics classes each morning and I will try to catch up on my correspondence as well as do a little studying of Persian Art and Literature. I have yearnings to scribble but didn't bring the typewriter because this is my one chance to get rested and I realize that it is essential. Since I brought 30-odd books to read for the library I'll have plenty to do.

Late one afternoon I sat on a point overlooking a wide expanse of wheat fields. I could see the various processes enacted – a group of men, women and children cut the grain with sickles in one place – farther west I heard a young boy singing a monotonous, doleful tune as he rode a bar behind oxen who trampled loose the grains. He carried a tin scoop ready to prevent the animals from soiling the harvest. In the next field men winnowed the grain by tossing it into the air with wooden shovels. In the midst of the fields I saw a cluster of houses where the smoke of an outdoor fire indicated that someone was busy preparing supper for the harvesters.

We visited Dr. Arfea's father-in-law's garden. We walked across fields, climbed a stone wall and walked up a poplar shaded walk with almond, peach, apple and apricot orchards on each side. His house is a modern looking building on top of a slope surrounded by furiously blooming dahlias. We sat on grassy lawn, had water and melon and cookies.

Mahmoud's father visited us – interesting black browed face, an early Christian convert.

Thursday we walked down to the bus stop, passing a walled place where a man was making mud brick for his new home, digging down his own land to get his building material – all except one little patch which was brightly abloom with flowers, now 4 or 5 feet above the level of the rest of the property. I couldn't help but moan over the top soil that had gone into bricks and wonder if anything would grow in the land that he had left himself. Perhaps he didn't plan to grow anything, especially, since his plot was not very large.

We left the bus at a wide traffic circle. Along the main street were curbside gardens with morning glories, cockscomb, zinnias and marigolds. We walked down into the bazaar where we bought material and embroidery thread to do a bridge table cloth in the Gujarati stitch

Mr. Beach taught Wetherill. A friend of Bob Bucher's led us to the old covered bazaar to get rope. We watched men weaving course bands of goat hair. Got a black and white goat's hair saddle bag and *aujideh* (native shoes like *giveh* but with leather stitched with cord on the soles – not so slippery as *giveh*). Then went to a pottery shop to buy Hamadan's famous product with its turquoise blue glaze, less often in green or yellow. Finally we were taken up to loft where we saw pottery horses, camels and fat tailed sheep. Got black pottery ends for a hubble bubble pipe, etched with white, to make interesting candlesticks. Os added a brown felt hat like villagers wear to his collection, rather a high crown with no brim. Came home in a taxi – ran out of gas and carried our many bundles across the fields for half a mile.

On Friday, four Cressons started off for the Citadel on a hill northeast of town. Its history is unknown but it was a fine site for defense with a good view over the city. There is nothing left but bare mounds to indicate where a tower and some of the reputed seven circled walls were. Each circle was supposed to have been a different color, with the two highest and innermost being of silver and gold.

Went down into the city thru tiny narrow walled-in streets. Turning a corner, Wetherill and I came upon a fuzzy haired woman squatting beside a child. When Osborne followed us, she saw him and squawked and ran for her doorway. I looked around and a group of chadorred women behind whom she hid laughed with me. A woman is supposed to have her hair covered even though many women allow their faces to show. There are not so many un-chadorred women in Hamadan as in Tehran.

The *kuchehs* were swept for it was Friday – looked very neat. Visited Mordecai and Ester's tomb though the smiley, bald little man did not have the key to let us in – a stone door barred the way. Went home in a *droshky*. In the afternoon we walked across fields to the Hamadan Lion where women pour oil on its head and pray to have children. Didn't look much like a lion except for one haunch. Perhaps praying hands have rubbed the carving smooth for there is none of the perfection of detail – it's not much more than a lump. Did see two carved pieces of what might have been legs or pedestals lying loose under the body of the Lion. Two boys were perched on its back when we went to see it, carving their initials on the hump of its shoulders! Such treatment for the remains of one of Alexander's monuments, as it is supposed to be.[80]

We went down to see the tomb of Mordecai and Ester again.[81] It is in a small shrine which you enter thru a smaller door. There were many visitors in an outer room with three tiers of votive candles burning – very hot. There is a very low door into the room of the tombs. One has to bend double to get thru so everyone enters in a reverent attitude. The filigree wooden cases are covered by block print cloths and embroidered velvet. Ester must have been a tiny lady and Mordecai not very tall if the sarcophagi were their full size. In another room there was a brass bound box holding the words of Moses, we were told. We didn't realize we were supposed to take off our shoes. Very abashed.

On the way home Montazemi stopped for a paper. A glass eyed man sidled up, reaching about to my shoulder, and asked what we were doing. When Montazemi returned the man said we should go to the police and show our residence permits. (We had already told the police of our arrival and showed our documents.) Montazemi told the slick, evil looking fellow that if he wanted to see our papers he could come out to Nur Mahal next day – we were too busy to come to town. We figured the man was merely an officious minor official for he never came out, nor did he make any effort to detain us when Osborne hailed a taxi and we got in, quite ignoring him.

The next day, leaving Joy to nurse a sore throat, seven of us walked down to the bus line. Got a bus to the center of town, called the Maidan, with a statue of the Shah in the middle of the circle. While

80. This is one of the lions carved on Alexander's orders to honor his friend and second-in-command, Hephaestion, who died in Ecbatana in 2342 years ago. During the Parthian period the lions were placed at the city gate.

81. The tomb has long been an important pilgrimage site for the Jewish people of Iran. It is traditionally associated with Esther, the Jewish wife of King Ahasuerus, sometimes identified as Xerxes who died in 465 BCE. Esther and Mordecai, a cousin who raised her, intervened with the king to save the Jewish community of Susa, the capital in southwestern Iran. Since the tomb is newer than that, it is thought to perhaps be associated with another Jewish queen, Shushandukht, the wife of King Yazdegerd who reigned from 399 to 420 CE in Ctesiphon, 22 miles south of Baghdad. Shushandukht was a great help to her people and is known to have established Jewish communities in several Persian cities.

Bob bought smoked salami we waited and realized that we already had a few friends in town. Numerous droshky and taxi drivers bowed and greeted us!

Took a bus up toward the mountains until we came to a small village, Abawsabad, at the end of the line. Bob pointed out that on the bus were Jewish people on their Saturday holiday, Muslims, Christians and a Zoroastrian. Then we started walking up the valley toward Ganj Namch ["treasure epistle"]. Our route was a shaded road at first with a continual up grade. Stopped to wash our hands and soak our bandanas at a cut-off where a man had charge of valves turning part of a mountain stream aside into an irrigation ditch. Then on again into a field of rocks along a sandy path. It was hot and glaring in the narrow valley though the *jube* (ditch) across the way made some greenery on the rocky hillside. We stopped at a spring for water and found two turtles about 8" across. They looked just like the stones around them. From there it was not far to a *chai-hawna* and then thru a willow grove until we saw the elaborate carved tablets of Darius and Xerxes high on the side of a cliff across the way.

Written in cuneiform in three languages (Farsi, Elamite and Babylonian), this is a first-rate billboard of great antiquity. Darius' tablet reads:

"A great god is Ahuramazda, who created this earth, who created yonder heaven, who created man, who made peace for man, who made Darius king, the one king of many, the one ruler of many. I am Darius the Great King, the King of Kings, King of the countries which have many peoples, King of the great earth even to afar, the son of Hystaspes, the Achaemenian."

Xerxes had one carved, placing it on the right and a little lower down than that of his father. He used the same wording, inserting his name in place of Darius'. These two tablets provided a key to cuneiform writings, making it possible to decipher other inscriptions. [The carvings must be about 2500 years old, since Darius died and Xerxes succeeded him in 485 BCE.]

This was on a hill above a lovely mountain stream and we enjoyed picnicking where we could look across to those old writings.

Bob, Osborne, Os, Wetherill and Montazemi went to see the

falls above. Bob had a shower in the icy water. O, O and M climbed back over the high peak where the tablets were and kept us waiting quite a while – I was mad.

It was much easier going back, the down grade didn't seem as steep as it did going up. A bus was waiting and left soon after we arrived. Among the passengers was a man carrying a child with trachoma eyes all sticky and pussy as well as a scabby head. We all waved the flies off us vigorously as long as we were in that bus. When we got home we had rests, tea and baths.

Hamadan is famous for honey as well as pottery. We got some in a big jar that reminded me of Arabian Nights on a smaller scale, though not too awfully small, at that, for we put 26 pounds of honey in it!

We were flossy and traveled home by hired car instead of bus. At one point after going over a big bump, seeing the driver looking under the car, Osborne asked if a spring had broken and was told, no – he was looking to see if honey was dripping out!

Chapter 32: The Caspian Sea

Letter: September 28, 1952; Holiday Letter, 1952
Diary: September 5, 1952; We Went to School in Tehran

On our return to Tehran from Hamadan we stayed only long enough to get a permit to go to the Caspian[82] for the rest of our vacation. Though we had thought we would try to get to the train early, as usual we made a wild Cresson dash down the platform at the last moment. (We are fairly orderly people but catching trains is different – we shave our time to the barest margin.)[83] We were surprised to see so many people on the train – a continental type with compartments and an aisle on one side. We had reserved four seats of the six in a compartment. The other two seats were occupied by a soldier, his tiny wife and four children. Needless to say we bunched up a bit to give them space.

Our traveling companions proved to be most pleasant – He was an army officer returning to his post after ten days in Tehran attending a funeral. She couldn't possibly have been much over 25 though her eldest daughter was 11. They did not speak English so we had to use what we could of Farsi, and got along very well. Wetherill and Os have improved this summer though we don't get enough practice to be much good, any of us.

When we first started we crossed a plain that soon became a sandy desert rising high with red eroded crags quite near the train track. We were no sooner underway than the family began ordering and eating. They had tea and bottles of water, cookies and sherbet and limes which the children sucked without benefit of sugar. I marveled at the digestive fortitude the youngsters exhibited. Then at 12 lunch started. Not being hungry yet we sat opposite them watching the process. The waiter, who scurried continually from 8:40 AM in Tehran to 7:10 PM when we left the train, brought heaped plates of chalau kabob.

82. The Caspian Sea is the largest lake in the world, half again larger than all the five Great Lakes taken together. The water is about a third as salty as ocean water. It is surrounded by Iran, Azerbaijan, Russia, Kazakhstan and Turkmenistan.

83. Rebecca leaves it for the reader to notice that perhaps the one who enjoyed the rush was setting the timing. She liked to get there early and savor the moment.

The father and mother admonished the children to use their forks and spoons, but there were not enough utensils to go around and even the four-year-old ate adeptly with her hands. We suspected they were more accustomed to the age-old finger use than spoon and fork. Littering the floor were bits of rice, meat too tough for little teeth, fig skins, melon rinds, broken cookies and pieces of bread. We were relieved when a cleaner came with a short broom and swept up the floor.

We got out at every stop and made many friends. At one point everyone went to a spring to get water. So gay and excited. At another stop the eldest daughter got out and just before the starting whistle blew Osborne called out, "The girl has fallen into the *hoze*." Every station had a pool for washing and drinking. It was 5 or 6 feet deep and fortunately when Farishah fell in there was a man close by to haul her out for she did not know how to swim. Os and Osborne went out, we pulled the curtains and got her into dry clothes with my coat to keep her warm for we were heading into the mountains.

The ascent was steady but gradual and the road bed smooth. Again and again we looked out to see two or three levels of track below us. Wetherill, with pencil and paper, kept a tally of the 94 tunnels we passed thru!! The soldier, the little mother and the children learned Os' chant, "One coming up!" and they vied with each other to be the first to sing it out as we approached yet another tunnel – and how do you suppose they are ever to use that phrase?! They leaned far out of the open window waving their arms and eventually even I stopped expecting a tearing streamliner to decapitate them for it was a single track most of the way.

It was thrilling when we had passed thru the tunnel at the top, 3,000 feet above Tehran. It took 4 minutes and 5 seconds to go thru and when we came out the scenery was different for there was immediate evidence of more rainfall and as we went rapidly down, snaking along a narrow valley, and within a surprisingly short time we found ourselves at the bottom looking up to where we had been.

Our friends called our attention to the astounding "Pul-i-Breek" (Brick Bridge) over which we had passed without realizing it. It spanned a narrow valley, high in the air and it is reported that when the "Old Shah" (Reza Shah, the founder of the Pahlavi dynasty) first crossed the bridge he made the construction engineer stand beneath it so that if the Shah's train fell the engineer should be killed, too.

The mountains became greener, the valleys terraced and cultivated. Haystacks were raised on platforms to keep them above the winter snows and the dampness of the fields.

By dusk we came to the rice country and rain. All along the valley were little shelters guarding small rice patches. They were raised 3 or 4 feet above the grain and covered with mats, some tent like and covered on two sides, others, more poorly protected with a single mat windward. Numerous fires built on the platforms silhouetted the figures of men crouched over their evening meal.

We stood at the windows, breathless at the beauty flashing across our vision like stereopticon slides as we sped down to the sea. It was thrilling – the depth of the valley – the colors – small villages – clouds drifting – dramatic blackness of tunnels cutting it off and opening up.

It was dark when we got to Sari. A trainman who had made friends with the children directed a coolie to take our two heaviest bags and guide us to a car to take us on an hour's drive to Babolsar by the sea. The driver asked 65 Tomans [$13] since we were foreigners but we were prepared knowing we should not pay more than 25. Osborne offered 15T and I stood by in fear we might miss a ride, being a ghastly poor bargainer, and was much relieved when the driver suddenly agreed to 20T. Our bags were grabbed and Osborne's pen nearly pick pocketed and we were all four in a good Dodge sedan with two other passengers, the driver and a cleaner before we knew it.

We got to the Pensión Peniance of a Russian refugee couple in good order. Then Os had a screaming nightmare in middle of night which brought out all the other guests who were residing in the gatehouse with us.

We ate on the second-floor porch of the main house overlooking the beach, battling bees every morning when we tried to spread jam on our bread.[84] Ghastly service, Ali plunking our food in front of

84. The woman who owned the pensión was tall and very heavy. At breakfast she put saucers of grape jam on the tables and then came back periodically to mash visiting

us and never keeping the courses straight. Few vegetables but chicken almost always twice a day.

Our pensión overlooked the water and what a thrill it was for Wetherill and Os who have had such an arid life! However, within a few hours Os was wheezing – the first trouble he has had in 2¾ years. He insisted upon staying and when the weather cleared he was able to make out if he did not exercise very much.

The Caspian is not as salty as the Atlantic and we missed the salt smell but some days it was a beautiful color. We took a rowboat-gondola across river to a point and walked up to where people gathered to bathe. One man rowed and a little boy poled at the stern. Wetherill learned to row and even pole and she and a boy won a race with another boat one day. We sometimes took the boat out to sea and around the point.

At the beach there were women bathing, some in bathing suits, and local people farther down, some of the women in dresses and long black pants with shawls over their heads even in the midst of the breakers. Once we went quite far out to see an iceboat that was anchored off shore. Days went by with swimming, reading and eating. We all turned a good shade of brown.

We met Dr. Sahleh and family. Wetherill had met the two older boys at her first formal party just before we left Tehran. Their mother is American, they have both American and Iranian names, Robert Baizad, 15, and Peter Kaivon, 14. They prefer being called by their American names and were awfully pleased to have Wetherill as an added attraction. Being good swimmers they kept close to her and saw she came to no harm.

Two days of rain at the end of our stay put Os in bad shape so we came home a day early. He cleared up as soon as we got into drier air.

The trip back by road was another thrilling experience. Even Osborne can't think of any road more spectacular. We soon left the almost tropical coast and drove thru a narrow canyon with rock walls rising fully 1000 feet above us. At the end of the canyon there was a

bees with a spoon and stir the concoction. Gradually the jam became thick with dead bees. She did it with great gusto, twinkling at the children.

waterfall which we passed five times before we had wound ourselves up to a point where we could cross into another valley.

We were ever so glad to have seen those sights, they are such a different part of Iran.

Chapter 33: Tabriz

Letter: March 7, 1953

If all goes as planned there will be quite an exodus for *No Ruz* – nine teachers and Anne and Jean Wild will go to Isfahan while our family and Margaret Wilson from Iran Bethel will go to Tabriz – she to see her grandchildren and we to see one more corner which we have missed. It will be good to get away for a little change. This has been a busy year, as much for the children as for their parents.

[Tabriz, a hub of the old Silk Road, is the key city on Iran's northwest frontier. At an elevation of 5000 ft, it is a favorite place to escape the summer heat. We went in the spring because we wanted to see it, and our time in Iran was running out.]

Letter: March 25, 1953; We Went to School in Tehran

I was as up at 5:00 on Friday to get Anne and Jean ready to go to Isfahan with the single teachers. Batool's Hassan took them to the bus station and then returned for us because our bus did not leave until 7:00. We were ready when he came except that Os couldn't find his overcoat! His *pustin-cha*[85] and Kabul suit coat were just as warm so he went that way. We took a blanket and my fox skin cape and wished we had taken more. A small suitcase, shopping bag and lunch carton made our luggage easy to handle.

We got down to the bus station in plenty of time. When we arrived there were about fourteen buses getting ready to leave for various spots. The people were all gay and friendly in a true holiday spirit. The next day was the New Year – the first day of spring – and people were going to their native villages for the holiday. Osborne asked where the Tabriz buses were – two were making the trip that day – and we were quite proud of ourselves because the children and I could read enough to find our names on the seat chart that was tacked to the bus window. Margaret Wilson, whose son and family are missionaries in Tabriz, and

85. A short coat or vest of sheepskin with the fur on the inside, the soft leather exterior often covered with embroidery.

Harriet Pease, who has been there for 32 years, were traveling with us. It was very pleasant to have the old timers along to point out things of interest. They were good travelers and I was much interested to see how well they knew how to prepare. Margaret came with a vacuum bottle, boots, and a sleeping bag to keep her feet warm. Harriet had Dramamine for the road is rough and winding. Wetherill and Osborne used the Dramamine for they have the queasy tummies of the family. Os and I got along beautifully without it. The people on the bus were more friendly than we have often found Iranian travelers to be.

There were many buses ready to leave and they got off on time, too. All our passengers were settled and we said Father's "Here we go-oo-o" at two minutes before seven! Buses in Iran leave on time and woe betide the latecomer. Made good time to Qazvin, arriving at 9:15. Stopped a short time at Takestan where the Hamadan road branches off. Noticed a housewife was using haystacks on the roof to spread her laundry out to dry. There were more trees on the plains after Takestan. Saw a woman on her roof watching the bus go by – she wore the village short pleated skirt and black pants.

From there we crossed a wide plain that was snow covered and hard on the eyes. Osborne and I were so tired that we dozed a great part of the way – as much as the bumpy road allowed for we couldn't rest our heads on the seats they bounced so. At Zanjan we stopped for lunch and a "rest stop."

The *chai-hawna* had a toilet so we didn't have to find a corner behind a wall but we joined the waiting crowd. Men and women waiting with aplomb for their turn at the single hole. There is no self-consciousness here about nature's needs, and the arrangement is far superior to American plumbing. Sometimes there are foot marks to show the correct place to stand and certainly having no seat to interfere makes things easier. *Mostara* (toilets) are usually quite clean.

We had lunch and Os bought a combination two bladed knife with a tiny fork and spoon attached. Zanjan is famed for its knives and filigree silver.

From Zanjan we started into the hills. At first they looked like pudding molds, with fluted humps, then they lengthened out and seemed like dinosaur hides. We saw an ancient mosque in the distance – quite an historic spot, evidently but I haven't had time to dig out its history – our informers were a little vague. We climbed on higher and higher, making one short stop for tea before dark and then not again until 10 o'clock, just before the highest pass that our companions were rather dreading not knowing how much snow might be up there. We went over the pass and its seven switch backs without any difficulty though we saw that oil trucks had to back and try a second time to get around the curves.

At Mianeh we stopped for tea but none of us wanted it except Harriet but she found too much of a crush waiting. We ate some supper in our laps just before dark and didn't stop until Bostanabad just before Shebli Pass. That is where we expected to show our documents but it was cold and dark and no one appeared. We had tea and then went on up Shebli which we crossed with no trouble. There was little snow. Arrived in Tabriz about 1 AM and there to meet us were Fred Wilson, Miss Johnson, with whom Harriet lives, and Arnold Schneider, with whom we would be staying! They had rented a room in the hotel and peeked out every time they heard a truck or bus. Arnold took us in a *droshky* (called *fitoon* in Tabriz) up to the hospital near the edge of town. It was cold.

Next day it snowed. Osborne attended to return bus tickets, police pass etc. The children and I stayed home and the Schneiders went New Year's Day calling. In the evening our children went with Arnold, Lois, Osborne and me to Frances Wooding's for dinner. All her arrangements and furnishings were very nice and her meal delicious. Biscuits and chicken.

The children had Sunday School with Lois, Arnold delivered a baby, Osborne and I toured the hospital. It is quite convenient but I thought what a fit some U.S. doctors and nurses would have over some of the equipment! It was worn, makeshift and a lot of it outdated but specklessly clean. We noticed the men patients all had their heads wrapped up – it is the custom to keep the head covered when in bed!

At noon we went to Fred and Betty Wilson's for dinner. Biscuits and chicken again! It was a treat and we didn't mention it nor object. Betty's house was very attractive, well arranged and her service nicely done. Found Fred had gone to Osborne's Haverford School for three years! Fred and Betty have very much to offer the mission in true friendliness and broadmindedness.

We all went to the home of the Schneiders' cook for tea celebrating *No Ruz*. We rode a long ways out, about five of us in each *droshky*. The son was waiting at the gate, the cook just inside. There was a small courtyard and we entered the three-room house via a vestibule. The living room was spick and spandy with straight chairs all around. In one corner was a table ladened with food. Before every second chair were small tables with candies, nuts, plates and fruit knives. They brought in cups of tea and passed three or four kinds of cake and cookies. Osborne took pictures of the children and tried a timed indoor shot of the tea party. We were glad to go to one New Year's party but were even more glad not to have to go to twelve in one afternoon as the missionaries had to.

Went to 5 o'clock Vesper service where we saw Mr. and Mrs. Cree. We had met them in Tehran before they went to Tabriz, he as Point Four Agricultural Director. Fred showed an Easter movie and then we went to Jonnie and Harriet's for supper. I was awfully pleased with the children who were so mannerly and pleasant. Harriet sent a letter with notes for Tehran in which she said she had fallen in love with our nice children. It is so thrilling to hear things like that when we know they are true.

We had snow every day we were in Tabriz but Monday morning it was fairly clear and Lois took us shopping and touring. Most of the covered bazaar was closed but we did find a heavy blue silk with a changeable border – a comfortable cover really – which we thought Wetherill might use for an evening shawl in years to come. Os found a skull cap, Wetherill some wool sox, and I two squares of heavy silk for headscarves. People seemed much more friendly than in Tehran.

Then we looked at the lovely blue tile at the doorway of an ancient, crumbling mosque and went on to the huge "Ark" which was an ancient fortress. It towered, a shell three stories high with two great arched doorways looking out over the city. We couldn't get up to climb to the top because the door had been bricked up – the steps have crumbled away. There is a new marble monument to unknown soldiers under a roof in the middle of the fortress enclosure. We watched well diggers with their simple wooden pulley letting goatskin bags down about 84 feet for a man to fill with mud as he dug deeper.

Found when we stopped in a silver shop that prices were just as high as in Tehran. Purchased a pair of salt cellars in Tabriz-Armenian design and two sugar shells. I asked if we might see the workshop and went in to watch the workmen. One was a boy about 12 or 14 who bored holes in a plate which the man opposite him cut on to make an openwork design on the edge. Another man was buffing a bowl into gleaming smoothness. The fourth – evidently the master craftsman – sat nearest the smudged windows cutting the typical Tabriz design on some tea glass holders. He followed a simple outline which had been traced on the holder, filling in the design, all by hand. Each workman had a large leather apron attached to the table to catch the silver shavings. There was little light, no heat and no ventilation and I wonder about the health of the workers. When I look at our salt shakers I will think of those poor workmen, bent over their tasks.

After lunch we had tea with the Crees. They were kind enough to tell us that our attitude had been a great encouragement and standard for them. They are trying hard to do something worthwhile and Osborne told them not to worry if they didn't see the results – in this kind of situation you have to do your best and not expect the reward of any satisfaction other than that. Sometimes, then, you get a pleasant surprise.

Osborne and the children went to pay our respects to the American Consul and got in on a cocktail party where he met a Lancaster, Pennsylvania boy who knew friends of ours. We were going to have supper at Gloria Simpson's house but she was so late coming in from *No Ruz* visiting that she brought her soup over to the Schneiders and we ate together. Afterward we worked riddles until bedtime.

Tuesday it was dark, cold and cloudy at 5 AM when we got up. Lois got our breakfast and Arnold, Gloria and Mary walked the mile down to the bus station and waited to see us off. It was snowing by then and we were a bit apprehensive about the pass but we got over it without any trouble though it was slow going. The wind up there is apt to blow snow off the slopes onto the road even when it isn't snowing. The sun was just coming out as we started up the pass – it was gloriously gleaming and too hard to look at long. Most everyone was watching the road and it was noticeable how they relaxed when we were over the pass. There were many curves though few switch backs after the pass.

We had lunch at Mianeh. Osborne and Os went looking for a bathroom as soon as the bus stopped. Wetherill was furious that they left her behind. By the time I got out of the bus she had left me! I went thru an arch, across a little courtyard and looked at a group of men standing at the foot of some steps. I turned away but one of the men called me and pointed up the stairs. There on the balcony I found as is usual in Iran, men and women both waiting to use the same toilet. There isn't any ladies first about it either!

We had our sandwiches in a little cubbyhole with another family. They tried to force their food on us. It embarrassed us to refuse, perhaps we should have taken something and not eaten it. That would have been more polite. We gave them some candy. Didn't get any tea – the waiters were too busy. Not being hot, we didn't feel the need of it.

Afterwards, the hills and valleys rolled on and on until we came to a great flat plain and finally the Pudding Mold Hills. Stopped a short time at 5 PM in Zanjan but didn't get tea – too many others again. Had some supper in the bus and didn't stop until we got to Qazvin at 10 PM. Since curfew was on we couldn't get to Tehran so we went into the hotel and got a room with two beds – one single and one 3/4. We put the Osbornes in the bigger bed and the Rebeccas in the smaller and finally got our feet warm.

It was much too soon when a bell rang to warn us to get up. The electricity was turned off but Osborne got a lamp. He went down to find the bus gone – but it came back – and the cleaner came up to get us. He was pleasant and helped Os down the dark stairs.

On the road again, we watched the sky lighten and the sun came up. Demavand was rose-white and cone-shaped above the other mountains. It is quite an astounding sight, going up so majestically, so far above anything else. We arrived on our doorstep at 7:30 and Yeksabet gave us *pishki* (a Russian pastry) for breakfast. We were glad that we had gone to Tabriz.

Chapter 34: Back to America

Diary: June 22, 1953
Letters: August, 1952 – June 18th, 1953

Tuesday, January 29, 1952.

There was a tug when Arthur Pack[86] wrote to Osborne asking him to become business manager of the Española Hospital!! They wanted him in April so we had to say that we couldn't come, but added that if they wanted us in 1953 we would consider; for Wetherill then should be Stateside to have her teeth straightened, and if we were there I would be able to concentrate on being a mother for the last years the children will be with us. But then we would have to leave Iran – wouldn't that be awful? The tug is both ways.

August, 1952.

[Rebecca explained the decision to leave Iran in a letter to her sister, Tiddo, written while at Babolsar on the Caspian:] The way you planned and wrote about Ret's operation was a masterpiece and I thoroughly agree that hush-hush is ridiculous and it is just as well to face the thing as it is. [Ret was her mother, Rebecca Edwards Shannon.] With all the problems that Ret has had, I wish this might not have been. I have been told that in a removal of cancer if it does not recur within five years, the operation has been successful. And there are better prospects for breast cancer which can be removed more easily than some internal types. We felt badly that all the arranging, support and encouragement fell to you and at a time when your job was especially heavy, too.

It has all brought our own decision to a head. We will plan to remain in the U.S. after this year instead of considering a return to Tehran. Of course, it means job hunting which is not easy at long distance. We had thought to try something near N.J. because Os had had no asthma for 2¾ years but when we got up here at the Caspian

86. We knew Arthur and Phoebe Pack when we lived in Española NM, 1947-1949. In 1945 they donated a hospital to Española. The Packs owned Ghost Ranch which they gave to the Presbyterian Church in 1955 for use as an education and retreat center.

he began to tighten up. Since he had stood at an open window most of the train trip up and caught the cold that laid me low the day after we returned from Hamadan, there were definite complications but it was disappointing to have it happen the first time we came to a damp area. Now we don't know whether he could battle the climate of the eastern seaboard or not.[87]

Osborne felt pretty low since it limits his choice of job so rigorously if he has to look only in a dry area. There seem to be so few opportunities for things of his interest in the southwest. He would like to continue school affiliated business management which he has enjoyed. The business end is more to his taste than teaching though he rather enjoys that, too, and he feels education answers his desire for a "constructive" type of work. He would like to get into a Quaker school so the children could be in that atmosphere. I hope he can get a job adequate enough so that I can return to my own field of motherhood and housewifery with perhaps time to do some scribbling in hopes I can earn some money for Ret's needs and develop a source of income for emergencies – but a source that won't also be an irritation and won't take me from my primary job of my own children.

We enjoy the interest and stimulation of living in a different country, we know that we will never again have two servants and such an elaborate house and there is a certain stability in the Mission but our position is rather anomo (don't know how to spell it!) [anomalous] since we are not Presbyterian and though people have been very decent we are occasionally made to feel as outsiders. It is rarely an intentional thrust so we don't take it personally. But we definitely feel that since we thought we should not leave for Afghanistan while Mother Cresson was ill that even more so, we should be nearer to Ret, especially since Wetherill and Os are her only grandchildren and you are the only one to carry the burden of her care.

When we return to Tehran I'll enclose a check for the balance of the *Geographic* money – we gave a tenth of it to the south Tehran

87. Because of my asthma we moved from New Jersey to New Mexico when I was 3, then to Asia, and to Arizona until I was 15. At that point we moved to Philadelphia and I was fine. The doctors in NJ said I would outgrow the asthma and I did. In the meantime it limited our choices of where to live, but this led us to some wonderful places.

slum work – to help out in Ret's expenses. She needn't know about it, that is why I thought it would be better to send it to you. This fall I'll try to get the other *Geographic* article written and hope to sell it, too. Osborne is getting a few pictures taken.

If Ret is feeling alright next summer wouldn't it be nice to go ahead with the European trip as we planned? I'd like so much for her to have that. I've thought so often, how nice it has been that she has had this time in her own home and in such enjoyable surroundings. Don't hesitate to let us know Ret's and your needs because we have the children's education funds upon which we can draw and when they go away to school I can go to work if need be.

[Rebecca's diary is silent between August and December. She never liked writing about conflict. I remember difficult arguments. One option was to return to Iran after a furlough year. Osborne would have work he was good at, and there was the excitement of cultural diversity in Community School, and we had learned a lot about living in Iran, and we enjoyed it. The other option was to go to America, where job prospects were uncertain, but Wetherill and I would be exposed to a normal teenage environment, and our family would have cultural and educational opportunities, and more contact with Quakers, and less stress from some of the strongly motivated missionaries around us and the politics of Iran at that time. We had delayed our trip to Afghanistan because of the health of Osborne's mother, and now we might have to delay a return to Iran due to the Ret's health. It was a difficult decision.]

Monday, December 29, 1952.

Mr. Payne is trying to get us reservations on the French Line about Aug. 15-20. As soon as we hear we will let you know so Ret can be fixed up. We thought French Line would give the children a chance to practice their French on the stewards. We will have to take steps to see that Wetherill especially, who has had two years, will not forget what she has learned. Osborne and I don't have any language left for secrets!

Sunday, January 11, 1953.

Mr. Payne is making reservations for us on the *Isle de France* sailing from Southampton on Sept 14!!! He insists on making it Cabin Class – it is beneath the dignity of missionaries to travel Tourist Class! Ret, make yourself a reservation and begin to plan for the summer. School isn't out until June 20. We are thinking of going with our baggage to Beirut and then by train to Istanbul so that we can see more of what Turkey looks like. It may be there won't be enough time.

Tuesday, February 3.

We have had our first sniff at a job. Sidwell Friends School in Washington may need an assistant headmaster and math teacher but there is no certainty yet and we may have to wait a month or two to hear. It would be sort of fun to be in Washington again though housing would be a problem.

Os is urging a place in the country but Osborne doesn't warm up to that. Actually it might be the best bet for Os in that climate but there is no use considering housing until we have a job! I am not planning to work and have begun talking up a mechanized house so that I will have some time to scribble. Life now is just plain too busy and exhausting. My blood pressure was up but two weeks of medication brought it down to normal.[88]

Tuesday, February 17.

Don't laugh – but we are now officially missionaries!!! We have been appointed as "Affiliated Missionaries" attached to Tehran Station. Osborne thought that it was the proper thing to do and Dick was anxious to have it go thru so that our reappointment to Community School would be facilitated should we ever choose to return.

Saturday, February 21.

Sidwell Friends School had already hired an Assistant Headmaster by the time Osborne's application got there. There might be an opening in the Math Department later. I was disappointed because

88. Medication successfully controlled Rebecca's high blood pressure for the rest of her life.

Osborne likes the administrative end. Oakwood Friends School in Poughkeepsie wrote Osborne that he sounded exactly like what they would need – in September next year! No other nibbles.

We will see if we can't arrange something like picking Ret up in Liverpool, seeing the lake district and Wales, London and maybe we could duck back to Dieppe if Andre Poulain is still there and sail from La Havre instead of Southampton. If you could land in France maybe we could see Brittany and then go to England and Wales.

Monday, February 23.

Well, I did nab Osborne for a chat about our travel schedule. We think we may take a plane to Beirut and a bus to connect with the Ankara train where Altay would meet us and conduct us to Istanbul. I favor a plane to Athens and Naples to save time and effort. He feels that it would be best if Ret could get a round trip on the French Line and meet us in France. *Inshallah* it all works as we hope.

I am going to begin packing in another month. Four months and we hope to be on our way!

Saturday, March 7.

When we get back from the Tabriz vacation I'll begin to pack, and am I beginning to wish we didn't have so many things?! Osborne and Wetherill tell me that I must pack the big jar we brought from Hamadan with our honey. It is huge and breakable.

Monday, April 13.

Haven't gotten anything packed yet but have done a lot of sorting and throwing away, and hope to begin putting things away before the week is out though that may be wishful thinking considering our schedule. There are a lot of extracurricular activities this week at school.

Monday, April 20.

Arthur Pack wrote with three job suggestions. We hurried to write to the Pasadena Branch of the American Friends Service Committee to see if Osborne could have a recently vacated job in Friends Indian work in Arizona. The other possibilities are the Tucson YMCA or a school Arthur is interested in near Tucson. Also Sidwell wrote to see if Osborne could teach a senior math course (including all the worst – calculus etc.) and physics.

What excitement last night! Chuck Swan brought in letters from both Ret and Tiddo. I had gone to bed early and woke up when Osborne came to bed so we read all the letters. We are tickled that you have gotten your reservation. Ours is not a definite location [Southampton or LeHavre] but an assurance that we will be booked on the *Isle de France* on August 14th.

We have just taken another step on our itinerary. Park Johnson promised, or rather insisted that he be allowed to inquire about boat reservations from Beirut to Izmir on June 25th or thereabouts.

We hope to get off from here exactly nine weeks from today. It sounds such a short time it gives me the shivers.

Tuesday, April 21.

I have one trunk partly packed but it hasn't been going ahead very fast. Now I must do some letter writing for Osborne.

Sunday, May 10.

I spent the day on business letters. Sidwell School in Washington D.C. think they would like Osborne to teach Physics and Senior Math and Pennington, N.J. thinks they might have housing if Osborne wanted to teach Math there. We still think AFSC [American Friends Service Committee] Indian work in Arizona would be first choice (partly for Os' health) but Pennington is so wonderfully close to Morristown and Sidwell has quite an international aspect with so many Embassy children. I <u>wonder</u> where we may land! Herrick Young, director of the International House Association thought he might dig up a job for Osborne. That would be interesting too.

Six weeks from tomorrow we hope to take off! Dick suddenly decided that I should have six weeks instead of four to pack up and I am now only a housewife and mother. I consider it more time than necessary but it was fun on Saturday to be home doing things that needed doing.

Monday, May 11.

We still don't know where we may be – Sidwell is still corresponding about a post in Washington, D.C. They have tentatively offered Osborne Senior Math and Physics. It would mean more work for Osborne because he hasn't taught Physics though he prepared to teach it this year – spent his whole vacation preparing the course! Pennington School in Pennington N.J. has also tentatively suggested that Osborne teach math there. It is a boys prep and has the advantage of being in a fine location for seeing Ret often and easily – and not too hard a trip for Tiddo either, I should judge, if we met you in Trenton. It doesn't have any special attractions other than that, whereas Sidwell is a Friends School, we could become acquainted with our own meeting [Friends Meeting of Washington D.C.]. We have lots of friends who will be coming and going and living in Washington but the climate would be tough on Os and we would probably feel that we should send him to Verde Valley School in Arizona after one year. I hate to have the youngsters away at school so early but we can't be too choosy. I wrote the first letters for Osborne way back last December and am just about ready to have some job breakthrough – it is awfully nuisanceful not to know where we can plan to be.

Wetherill and I were just talking about traveling clothes. We are getting some crinkle crepes made so that we can have clean clothes without ironing them and save regular cottons for special appearances when we see people we know! Mehri is making me some afternoon dresses since I was flat out of all my hand-me-downs. We are trying to combine various patterns so that my clothes won't all look alike. The few patterns we can get here are frightfully expensive. I have a black and white with a touch of blue which Wetherill thoroughly approves of (she is very decided in her tastes on dress matters – and quite good). She didn't much like my choice of a plain gray to wear with a white collar and cuffs but I think it will be rather neat if Mehri gets it made well enough. I hope to wear it to a cocktail party tomorrow, *Inshallah.* It will save my clothes considerably not to be in school because I can get away with wearing a dress two days at home but at school it had to be a clean one each morning.

Tuesday, May 19.

Our job prospects are still in a fluid state and we are just about ready to settle for ditch digging in order to be over the suspense. About our possessions – whatever you have is to stay with you. There will be other furniture to take care of us and just now, in the process of packing up, I would just about wish there wasn't a thing! I do enjoy things that have some meaning and attachment and beauty but not when I have to pack them.

Osborne brought over a letter from Pasadena Friends sending an application blank and writing a letter that we are a bit baffled by. Ed Sanders said that Osborne's letter to Dave Walden made them enthusiastic about Osborne and the whole family but he knew Osborne would want to meet two people in the Indian work and be seen by the Personnel Committee which he could do in mid-August. Then he asked for addresses en route from Tehran to New York. Why, we ask you.

My immediate reaction was "alright let's put all our eggs in that basket" and much to my surprise Osborne and Wetherill immediately felt the same thing. Os, bless him, took time to consider what it would mean if one or the other of the parties didn't like each other. I thought how much farther than Pennington, Arizona is but I do feel that it is essential that Osborne do the work he most wants to do and Arizona would be so much better for Os – perhaps we will have to arrange long visits rather than more frequent short ones.

So I guess that Osborne will be writing to Pasadena that he will abandon the other possibilities in hopes that the Indian work will materialize. There isn't much else that he can do and if something happens to the Indian job we will just throw ourselves at Mr. Pack's door and I bet he will turn up a job. He had two other suggestions besides the Friends work.

Wednesday, May 27.

With all four voting, we decided unanimously to wait until Osborne can interview with the Pacific Office of AFSC about the Indian work in Arizona. They don't make appointments sight unseen. So, rash as it may seem, we won't accept a job elsewhere until we have a chance at Indian work. It is farther away than we had thought to be but, of course, puts Os in a congenial climate and Wetherill says she would rather be in the Southwest than the East. It may mean of course that we get stuck without a job but Osborne says he guesses we are gamblers at heart. Os, strangely, was the one who thought the thing thru most carefully and only decided to favor it when he found that we could live a few months on our bank account. He is usually so impetuous that I was pleased to see him reason when he really wanted to go to Arizona.

It is with slightly sinking hearts that we realize there are less than four weeks left before we leave Iran. When we think that we won't be around to watch certain boys and girls develop, certain activities thrive and certain projects mature it gives us a low feeling. And then we plan a little more about our trip and are raring to go.

We will, barring accidents, be at LeHavre on July 24th. We don't know whether it would be best to take a little trip around Brittany and a quick squint at the Chateau country or go first to Paris. Perhaps the latter would be best, and then find out there about possible jaunts that would not tire Ret too much.

Mr. Payne is trying to push us around on our departure transportation. He was doing quite a job persuading Osborne to go to Beirut by bus – Osborne being quite anxious to see as much of this part of the world as possible – I was in the next room and ambled in to interfere. I don't want to lug Os over that desert country as a beginning for a long and tiring trip. It might ruin Os' whole trip and would yield comparatively little of interest whereas there is so much in Istanbul, Rome etc. At this point I am going to be stubborn and don't think that Mr. Payne will hold out against us when he finds it is no go.

Our counting the days is not taking the form that it usually does. To think – only three weeks and two days to do all the things and see all the people that we are going to want to do and see. It gives me a sick feeling. There are so many nice people.

Thursday, June 18, 1953.

This may be quite likely the last letter I write from Tehran! It seems unbelievable that the time before our departure is so short. Our plans are really shaping up since your letter of June 3 which took twelve days to get here. Much of our mail has evidently been lost. We hope that the application blank to Friends Service got thru.

To reiterate our schedule as far as planned: At 3:25 Monday, June 22 (your day) we take off by Air France with Betty Carr, her two girls [Deedee and Patty] and another Community School family, including one of our biggest problem boys! A number of people threaten to see us off though it means getting to the airport an hour before take-off in order to see us before we go into the Customs confines.

We will be in Beirut until Wednesday the 24th when we go to Istanbul where we will stay at the Bible House (!). The Buchers will be there for one day, with us, then we have seven days more after they leave. On July 2nd we hop down to Athens and on to Rome on the 4th. We are making contact with a New Mexican boy in Rome who is to receive his first priesthood orders a few days after we see him. From that point until we meet you twenty days later our route is indefinite but we hope to see Pompeii, Florence, Venice, Milan, do a circuit around Switzerland and perhaps take a bus to Paris.

We wrote the Paris hotel to expect all five of us from the LeHavre boat train on July 24th and asked Andre if we could see him on the 25th in Paris. Osborne would like to go back to Luneray where Andre's family will be staying but we will have to see how plans work out. Mr. Appleton, near London, offers us lodging in his house while we are there. He stayed with us last year and I think you will like him. It will be fun to be in a real English home rather than a hotel I think. Mr. Appleton is a former Missionary of the Anglican Church! We certainly have a variety of contacts, don't we? Of course we will have to try to get to the Eisteddfod[89] in Wales for a day or two.

This last week is getting busier as it goes along – Sunday at five was Baccalaureate, however it is spelled (the dictionary is packed). That evening Margie, Os and Wetherill went to a party at Patty Carr's house. Both girls wore "formals" and Wetherill looked like a dream in a white organdy with tiny red dots, a red sash and necklace. It was a thoroughly satisfactory party seemingly. Monday morning our boxes went to the Mission office and Tuesday I went down to see them thru

89. The Welsh national festival of the arts. Ret's grandparents were music loving Welsh immigrants.

Customs. Not a box or trunk was opened except to put in a late gift which was a heavy stone vase I didn't want to lug thru Europe. The Buchers, Hoffmans and McNair's trunks went with ours. That evening we had supper with John and Ruth Elder. Wednesday I did letters and Osborne gave exams.

Today we are due at the Embassy Residency for a farewell to the Carrs. Should be dressing this minute. Tomorrow is a humdinger: Commencement at 10. Quiet Time at 11:30. Lunch with one of the students, tea at an Iranian home and the prom at the Darband Hotel! Saturday Wetherill has a swimming party and luncheon, Chuck Swan leaves, Rob Warne has a party and there is a square dance!

Monday, June 22, 1953.

It didn't seem real at all when the day of our departure arrived. It was hot and we had much to do. I worried about getting all the clothes in the bags. I put the oldest in last and actually had room enough. Then we took our bags downstairs to weigh them. Our second largest bag was put on the scale. Os and I looked at it and gasped – we read it as 43¾ kilos and that was almost as much as two of us could have. We had done a trial weighing and thought we had space enough. I began wondering what had happened and how I could start eliminating big items. Then Os realized we were reading from the wrong side of the weight. I shook for half an hour afterward.

Osborne and Os took the bags down to the Air France office while Wetherill and I did last minute things like sorting old clothes, wrapping gifts for the servants etc. Mrs. Goldenberg came in to say goodbye. Had lunch with the Irvines – Dick was as usual late. We ran right off to change and were assembled when Mr. Payne came with Chuck. Got off at 2:15 on schedule.

[Many of the people named in this chapter were our special friends. Some had worked for us and were part of our family. Others were Community School students, Presbyterian mission staff, and a variety of people we met during our two years in Tehran.]

Mike Gannett and Charlotte were at the airport along with the Larsens, daSilvas, Parks, Mooshie, Fuad and Alfred. Mr. Payne hurried us into customs which was tantalizing because the busload that were coming to say farewell had not arrived. We would only be able to wave to them thru a window and at a distance. Customs inspection had its moments. First thing the inspector dragged out our leftover Afghan currency. It was registered in Osborne's old passport which he had in his briefcase but couldn't find. The inspector skipped that and went on to my Afghan purse which looked like a trunk. The poor man came up with some tampons I had dumped in at the last moment. I didn't know how to explain them and called to Mr. Payne. Both men were slightly thrown and the inspector didn't do a very thorough job on the rest of the inspection.

The Carrs went out to the plane first, then Chuck and John and we trailed along at the end. We must have looked odd. Os carried his violin, Wetherill nothing, Osborne his briefcase and I had the Afghan shopping bag plus all the coats which I had been holding onto in the confusion. We must have seemed quite typically Iranian with the woman trailing along carrying the biggest burden. There was a huge crowd – lots of school children, Batool, Mariam, Yeksabet, Navart, John and Ruth Elder, Dickin and so many people with whom we wished we might have had a last word. Bless them – they stood in hot sun in a packed jam for most of an hour. They cheered us, took our pictures and called, "Yankee go home!" to which Osborne replied, "We are!" I was first up the steps and when I turned to wave from the door so many hands were raised it made my heart thump to think how many friends we have.

Wetherill and I sat together and finally we took off. As the plane left the ground I heard her wail and turned to ask what was wrong. "I don't want to leave" she sobbed with great abandonment and grief. Not one of us who left Tehran felt excited or thrilled to go. My feeling was purely resignation. Wetherill controlled herself in the interest of seeing the airport slip away. It was bumpy and I was surprised at how many mountains we crossed. Bare and broken brown mounds with small patches of villages slipped away under us hour after hour. Betty Carr and I gabbed for a while, Patty and Os played cards, Chuck, Deedee and John played checkers and Wetherill dozed. We all ran to windows to see Baghdad on its big Tigris River bend. It looked like a model of a mud village. I was surprised at how brown the buildings looked. Syria seemed like just a continuation of the rest of the trip but as soon as we crossed the mountains into Lebanon the soil was redder, there were trees on the hills and the red tiled houses looked most interesting. We circled over the sea and came quickly into the airport.

Postscript

Our family went to Afghanistan and Iran to live with people who appeared to be different but who were fundamentally the same. Rebecca called it an experiment in outreach across cultures. We learned to overlook the differences in faces and clothing and how we eat and speak and write. Beyond it all we found people are similar in caring about children, in wanting good teachers, in liking to laugh.

After leaving Iran Rebecca and Osborne used the trip as an opportunity to visit Lebanon, Turkey, Greece, Italy, Switzerland, France, England and Wales. Her mother, Ret, joined us in France. (Rebecca was so excited waiting to see her mother that a button popped off her shirt!)[90]

Osborne found a job with the American Friends Service Committee (AFSC) in northern Arizona where he worked with Hopi and Navajo people. Then he became a high school teacher at Verde Valley School in Sedona, where Rebecca worked in the school office. Then, in 1956, we moved to Philadelphia, Osborne's ancestral home, where he taught in Friends Central School and Wetherill and I finished high school. For the first time we had a Quaker community nearby and we joined Radnor Friends Meeting. Rebecca became a weaver, volunteered in hospitals, and continued writing.[91] Osborne became a computer programmer working for a bank and then volunteered in that field at AFSC.

Wetherill married Allan Winder and had three children: Rebecca, Gordon and Owen. After growing up while moving around a lot, Wetherill settled in Iowa City, determined to give her children a stable home base with lots of opportunities for travel.

I visited and studied in Guatemala, Mexico and Kenya before teaching in Monteverde Friends School in the mountains of Costa

90. For more on this trip, see: Os Cresson, ed., *We Stood in Awe: Rebecca's Travel Diaries 1949 and 1953* (Iowa City, IA: Morning Walk Press, 2020).

91. Her writings, published and unpublished, are in the "Rebecca Shannon Cresson Papers" in the Friends Historical Library at Swarthmore College.

Rica. In 1974 Rebecca and Osborne visited and fell in love with the community, and the meeting, and the tropical setting. It worked out well and they lived in Monteverde for the next 22 years. I lived with them a lot of the time, and Wetherill and the grandkids visited regularly. Finally, Osborne passed away on the eve of their 60th wedding anniversary, and Rebecca a year later.

While we were in Iran, Rebecca had mused on death and life:

Diary: Notes; We Went to School in Tehran

South of Tehran are the ruins of Ray, built after the time of Alexander. A great and beautiful city, it once boasted 500 public baths, until it was destroyed by Genghis Khan. We went picnicking in the vicinity and climbed around the remains of the city wall. There is a spring nearby where rugs are brought to be washed. An ancient bas relief is on the rocky cliff above the pool.

We ate our picnic supper at what might sound like a ghoulish spot – beside the Tower of Silence where the Zoroastrians used to leave the bodies of their dead to the vultures. The children looked with calm at the bones and hunted the darkening sky for the raptorial birds. The view over the brown and green valley toward Tehran was wide, quiet and beautiful. As darkness grew the city lights came winking on at the base of the bold Elburz Mountains, and they rivaled the glory of the stars.

On the way home we passed rows of one room houses. The families were all out of doors in the warmth of the July night. Some still sat around a central supper dish by the light of a lamp, eating with their fingers. Some had already rolled themselves in their blankets or shawls, their heads completely covered. There was one family group of several men and a young woman intently watching a tiny girl showing how well she could stand alone.

During Quiet Time in our home in Tehran Christians, Bahais, Moslems, Jews, Zoroastrians and others spoke of reaching out in a loving way to the Light in every person. This is the way Rebecca and Osborne lived, and it is a good example for all of us.

Glossary

BURQA (BURR-kah). A robe that fully covers the woman, with an embroidered window.

CHADOR (cha-DOOR). A shawl worn over the head and shoulders that can be pulled across the face for more privacy. Words for articles of clothing can mean different things in different countries.

CHAI (CHAI). Tea; what every Iranian drinks, again and again.

CHAI-HAWNA (chai-hah-NAH). Teahouse where travelers rest and local men socialize.

CHALAU (chi-LOW). Plain rice, served with any of a variety of sauces spread over the top (see pilau).

DROSHKY (drowsh-KEY). Four-wheeled horse drawn carriage used as a taxi in Iran.

FARDA (far-DAH). Tomorrow (often hypothetically).

FARSI (far-SEA). The Persian word for the Persian language spoken in Iran, Afghanistan, and Tajikistan.

GIVEH (give-AY). Iranian sandal with a woven top made of fine knots of string and a leather sole.

HOZE (HOSE). Pond or pool.

INSHALLAH (in-shah-LAH). God willing.

JUBE (JEWB). Ditch.

KUCHEH (ku-CHEH). Alley.

MAJLIS (maaj-LEES). Iranian parliament.

MAWST (MAWST). Yogurt.

NAWN (NAWN). Whole wheat bread, baked in large thin platters with a rolled edge; the staff of life in Iran.

NO RUZ (NO ruze). New Year's Day, on the first day of spring; a time of much celebration.

PILAU (pih-LOW). Traditional rice dish in which the ingredients are mixed with rice and then cooked together. (see chalau.)

SHALOOK (shah-LUKE). Riot, demonstration or other disturbance.

TOMAN (toe-MAHN). The currency of Iran in 1952, equivalent to about 20¢ (U.S.). One Toman equaled 10 Rials, and one Rial equaled 20 Shahi.

Bibliography

Rebecca's Writings (unpublished except as shown)

American Family in Afghanistan. *The National Geographic Magazine*, vol. CIV, no. 3, September 1953, pp. 417-432.

Iran Diary, 1951-1953.

Iran Letters, 1951-1953.

Speech to Federated Women, 1955.

The House at 51 Howellville Road, 1967.

We Felt Their Kindliness: An American Family's Afghan Odyssey 1949-1951. Os Cresson, ed., Haddonfield NJ: Emerald Pademelon Press, 2003; 2nd edition, Iowa City IA: Morning Walk Press, 2019.

We Lived in Turbulent Tehran. *The National Geographic Magazine*, vol. CIV, no. 5, November 1953, pp. 707-720.

We Stood in Awe: Rebecca's Travel Diaries 1949 and 1951. Os Cresson, ed., Iowa City, IA: Morning Walk Press, 2020.

We Went to School in Tehran, 1953. (Rebecca's original manuscript for the *National Geographic* article, above.)

Note: Rebecca's writings are in the "Rebecca S. Cresson Papers" at Friends Historical Library of Swarthmore College.

Iranian History and Culture:

Abrahamian, Ervand. *A History of Modern Iran*. NY: Cambridge University Press, 2008.

Amanat, Abbas. *Iran: A Modern History*. New Haven, CN: Yale University Press, 2017.

Axworthy, Michael. *A History of Iran: Empire of the Mind*. NY: Basic Books, 2016.

Axworthy, Michael. *Iran: What Everyone Needs to Know*. NY: Oxford University Press, 2017.

de Bellaigue, Christopher. *Patriot of Persia: Mohammad Mossadegh and a Tragic Anglo-American Coup*. NY: HarperCollins, 2012.

Daryaee, Touraj. *The Oxford Handbook of Iranian History.* NY: Oxford University Press, 2012.

Ebadi, Shirin. *Iran Awakening: A Memoir of Revolution and Hope.* NY: Random House, 2006.

Foltz, Richard C. *Spirituality in the Land of the Noble: How Iran Shaped the World's Religions.* Oxford, UK: Oneworld, 2004.

Heiss, Mary Ann. *Empire and Nationhood: The United States, Great Britain, and Iranian Oil, 1950-1954.* NY: Columbia University Press, 1997.

Katouzian, M. A. Homayoun. *The Persians: Ancient, Medieval and Modern Iran.* New Haven CT: Yale University Press, 2010.

Katouzian, Homa and Shahidi Hossein, eds. *Iran in the 21st Century: Politics, Economics and Conflict.* NY: Routledge, 2008.

Keddie, Nikki R. & Richard Yann. *Modern Iran: Roots and Results of Revolution,* Updated Edition. New Haven CT: Yale University Press, 2006.

Kinzer, Stephen. *All the Shah's Men: An American Coup and the Roots of Middle East Terror.* Hoboken, NJ: John Wiley & Sons, 2008.

Lonely Planet & Simon Richmond, et al. *Lonely Planet Iran* (Travel Guide). NY: Lonely Planet, 2017.

Mackey, Sandra. *The Iranians: Persia, Islam, and the Soul of a Nation.* NY: Dutton, 1996.

Moaveni, Azadeh. *Lipstick Jihad: A Memoir of Growing up Iranian in America and American in Iran.* NY: Public Affairs, 2005.

Molavi, Afshin. *The Soul of Iran: A Nation's Struggle for Freedom.* NY: W. W. Norton, 2002.

Nafisi, Azar. *Reading Lolita in Tehran: a memoir in books.* NY: Random House, 2004.

Satrapi, Marjane. *Chicken with Plums.* NY: Pantheon Books, 2006. (autobiographical comic book)

Satrapi, Marjane. *Persepolis 1: The Story of a Childhood.* NY: Pantheon Books, 2003. (autobiographical comic book)

Satrapi, Marjane. *Persepolis 2: The Story of a Return.* NY: Pantheon Books, 2004. (autobiographical comic book)

Sciolino, Elaine. *Persian Mirrors: The Elusive Face of Iran.* NY: Free Press/Simon & Schuster, 2005.

Secor, Laura. *Children of Paradise: The Struggle for the Soul of Iran.* NY: Riverhead Books (Penguin Random House), 2016.

Semati, Mehdi, ed. *Media, Culture and Society in Iran: Living with Globalization and the Islamic State.* NY: Routledge, 2008.

Children's Books About Iran – Nonfiction:

Adl, Shirin. *I is for Iran.* London: Frances Lincoln Children's, 2011.

Donaldson, Madeline. *Iran* (Country Explorers Series). Minneapolis, MN: Lerner, 2010.

Kenney, Karen Latchana. *Iran* (Essential Library Countries of the World Series). North Mankato, MN: ABDO Publishing, 2011.

Bilings, Patricia & Fatih Erdogan. *Friends (English-Farsi)* (My First Bilingual Book Series). Chicago, IL: Milet Publishing, 2018.

National Geographic. *1001 Inventions and Awesome Facts from Muslim Civilization.* Washington DC: National Geographic, 2012.

Children's Books About Iran – Fiction:

Ahmadi, Ahmadreza. *Alive Again.* UK: Tiny Owl, 2017.

Balouch, Kristen. *Mystery Bottle.* NY: Hyperion, 2006.

Beh-Rang, Samad. *The Little Black Fish.* Bloomington, IN: Author House, 2008.

Climo, Shirley. *The Persian Cinderella.* NY: HarperCollins, 1999.

Javaherbin, Mina. *The Secret Message.* NY: Scholastic, 2010. (based on poem by Rumi)

Kalantari, Parviz. *Tahmineh's Beautiful Bird.* UK: Tiny Owl, 2015.

Laird, Elizabeth. *Pea Boy and Other Stories from Iran.* London: Frances Lincoln Children's, 2009.

Laird, Elizabeth. *Shahnameh: The Persian Book of Kings.* London: Quarto, 2014.

Napoli, Donna Jo. *The Earth Shook: A Persian Tale.* NY: Hyperion, 2009.

Vafaiyan, Marjan, Azita Rassi and Jalal al-Din Rumi. *The Parrot and the Merchant.* UK: Tiny Owl, 2017.

Index

Three books are available based on the writings and photos of

REBECCA SHANNON CRESSON and

OSBORNE COATES CRESSON

We Felt Their Kindliness: An American Family's Afghan Odyssey 1949-1951
It Made My Heart Thump: Rebecca's Letters From Iran 1951-1953
We Stood in Awe: Rebecca's Travel Diaries, 1949 and 1953

All income from these books will be donated to the
American Friends Service Committee
or used to publish and market additional copies of the books.

These books are published and distributed by
MORNING WALK PRESS, Os Cresson, editor
1 Oaknoll Court – Apt. 317, Iowa City, IA 52246
oscresson1@gmail.com, 319-512-1199

American Friends Service Committee

The American Friends Service Committee (AFSC) is a Quaker organization that promotes lasting peace with justice, as a practical expression of faith in action. Drawing on continuing spiritual insights and working with people of many backgrounds, they nurture the seeds of change and respect for human life that transform social relations and systems.

AFSC was founded in 1917 during World War I to give young conscientious objectors ways to serve without joining the military or taking lives. They drove ambulances, ministered to the wounded, and stayed on in Europe after the armistice to rebuild war-ravaged communities. Following that modest beginning, AFSC continued to respond in numerous ways to human suffering in Appalachian mining communities; on both sides of the Vietnam War; throughout the modern U.S. civil rights movement and public school desegregation; by working with you and economic development in Asia, Africa, and Latin America; and with numerous communities such as Native Americans, immigrants, migrant workers, prisoners, and low-income families in the United States on education and justice issues.

In 1947, along with British Quakers, AFSC received the Nobel Peace Prize, which recognized our work "...from the nameless to the nameless...." Today AFSC works in 15 countries around the world and 35 U.S. cities partnering with individuals and communities who are courageously working for justice and peace, often under the most challenging circumstances. Together, these efforts demonstrate the power of nonviolence to overcome injustice, violence, discrimination, and exploitation.

For more information please contact:
American Friends Service Committee, 1501 Cherry Street, Philadelphia, PA 19102. Telephone: 1-888-588-2372. www.afsc.org.

Made in the USA
Columbia, SC
02 March 2020

88599181R00157